IN AT THE DEEP END

SPEAKING ACTIVITIES FOR PROFESSIONAL PEOPLE

Vicki Hollett

Roger Carter

Liz Lyon

Emma Tanner

Oxford University Press
Walton Street, Oxford OX2 6DP

Oxford New York
Athens Auckland Bangkok Bombay
Calcutta Cape Town Dar es Salaam Delhi
Florence Hong Kong Istanbul Karachi
Kuala Lumpur Madras Madrid Melbourne
Mexico City Nairobi Paris Singapore
Taipei Tokyo Toronto

and associated companies in
Berlin Ibadan

OXFORD and OXFORD ENGLISH are trade marks
of Oxford University Press

ISBN 0 19 457204 8

© Oxford University Press 1989
First published 1989
Eighth impression 1995

Acknowledgements

The authors would like to thank EF
International Language Schools and all the staff
at EF Private Study Centre, Cambridge, for
their help in testing these materials. Their
professional advice and suggestions were
invaluable, and we couldn't have done it
without them.
All cartoons by Axel Scheffler. Other artwork by
Oxford Illustrators.

Typeset by Pentacor PLC, High Wycombe

Printed in Hong Kong

Contents

PART ONE: One-to-one

P = Preparation

P = Preparation

PART TWO: Pairwork

P = Preparation

PART THREE: Group work

Unit		Activities		Page	P	Time needed	Possible language work
23	Leading the group	1	Expressing opinions	87		***	Giving and asking for opinions Interrupting Giving reasons
		2	Leading a discussion	88	P	**	
		3	Giving reasons	88		**	
		4	Persuading	89	P	****	
24	Achieving consensus	1	Government priorities	91		***	Agreeing and disagreeing Generalizing Contrasting points
		2	Exceptions to the rule	93		***	
		3	The perfect manager	94		****	
25	Teamwork	1	Suggesting a course of action	95		**	Making suggestions Accepting ideas and raising objections Giving advice
		2	Advice	96		**	
		3	Solving problems together	96		*	
		4	Motivation	97		***	
26	Decision-making	1	The board meeting	98	P	***	Making proposals Making points Being non-committal
		2	Legal responsibility	100		**	
		3	Business ethics questionnaire	100		****	
27	Creative planning	1	Build your own utopia	103		****	Making suggestions Accepting ideas and raising objections Word building
		2	Scotch whisky campaign	103		****	
		3	The ideal workplace	105		****	
		4	A men's magazine	106		****	
28	Negotiations	1	True or false	107		**	Making conditions If/as long as/providing, etc. Explaining terms of business
		2	Discounts	107		**	
		3	A contract of sale	107		***	
		4	A bank loan	109	P	***	
		5	Union negotiations	109	P	****	

P = Preparation

Teacher's notes

Deep end strategy

This book is significantly different from traditional language courses. Students are launched in at the deep end and asked to perform speaking tasks in English without preliminary controlled practice activities. In this way the communicative needs of the individual students determine the content of the course.

Entry level

These materials are suitable for students at a wide range of language levels from lower intermediate to advanced. Many of the activities have also been used successfully with students at an elementary level of English.

Needs analysis

It is important to spend some time on the needs analysis to establish goals and priorities for study. It is the student who, with the help of the teacher, directs the selection of the activities. They can be performed in any order.

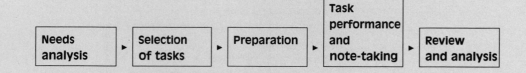

| Needs analysis | ▶ | Selection of tasks | ▶ | Preparation | ▶ | Task performance and note-taking | ▶ | Review and analysis |

Preparation

Some tasks are most useful when students have time to prepare before the lesson. These are marked **P** in the Contents chart. Students should make preparatory notes **but not write full sentences**. Key words generally work best.

Timing of activities

The time spent on each task will depend on students' needs and interests. Activities that are not relevant to particular individuals can be cut short or omitted. The pace of individual students varies so we have only given rough guidelines for the time needed.

*   Under 10 minutes
**   10–30 minutes
***   30–60 minutes
**** Over 60 minutes

Note-taking and recording

While students are performing a speaking task it is important to take notes for review and analysis at a later stage. Tape recorders and video cameras can be used, although it is often quicker and more efficient if the teacher writes notes. These can then be given to the students at the end of the session for further study.

Phrases

In these activities, teachers cannot know in advance exactly what students will want to say. The language they need to perform the tasks is unpredictable, so teachers should be ready to help the students by supplying language as required.

The phrases in the blue boxes accompanying the tasks will often serve as valuable reference, but they should only be used if they are appropriate for the ideas the students wish to express. **They shouldn't be forced on the situation if they don't sound natural.**

5

Review and analysis

Further work on the language points that arise during these exercises can be done in many ways and with a variety of materials. But very often the notes taken during the task can be a valuable source in themselves for analytical work. Students can be asked:

- to read the text, highlight new words and expressions and then construct new sentences with them
- to fill in blanked out words and phrases
  eg new vocabulary
     verbs
     prepositions
- to highlight particular words
  eg 3rd person 's' forms in the present tense
     adjectives
- to change verb forms
  eg present → past
     active   → passive
- to construct tables using words in the text
  eg irregular verbs
     words with common roots
     countable and uncountable nouns
- to precis the text
- to record the text, by reading or from memory
- to make notes on the text to be used for a further presentation.

This list covers some of the points you may wish to focus on when reviewing the tasks.

1 Tense work
   eg irregular verbs
      negative and question forms
      contrast and comparison of tenses

2 Functional work
   How different forms are used to:
   make offers
   give advice
   express opinions, etc.
   Also register and appropriacy work.

3 Holistic phrases
   Odd phrases, expressions and idioms that come up.
   eg She had to foot the bill.
      Have I got carte blanche on this?
      They're in the same boat.
      We'll leave it at that then, shall we?

4 Lexical families
   eg branch, division, section, department
      to sack, to fire, to dismiss, to lay off, to make redundant

5 Words with common roots
   eg to employ, employer, employee, unemployed, employment

6 Collocations

Words that frequently appear together.

eg market forces
    retail outlet
    postpone a meeting
    cancel an appointment

7 Over-used words

Students may be in the habit of using particular words rather a lot.

eg possibility, necessary, obliged to
    Teachers may wish to ban over-used words for a while to force students
    to try out alternatives.

8 False friends

English words that look similar to words in the student's language, but that translate differently.

eg sympathetic/likeable, sensitive/sensible, lucky/happy

9 Modal verbs

eg would/should, will/shall, must/have to
    Students may have difficulty forming questions and negatives or be
    confused about their different uses.

10 Pronunciation

Individual sounds (*eg* sink, think), word stress (*eg* economy, economic), intonation, weak forms, contractions, etc.

11 Prepositions

Prepositions used with time, direction and location. And all the prepositions that come before and after particular words that have to be learnt one by one.

12 Other grammatical work

eg countables and uncountables
    it is versus there is
    comparative forms

**PART ONE:
One-to-one**

The activities in this section have been designed specially for the one-to-one class. The teacher can often play a very active role in this lesson, working alongside the student to produce a good text for future reference. The student will be providing the ideas and thoughts that they want to convey, and the teacher will be:

- supplying unknown vocabulary and expressions
- helping the student select appropriate grammatical forms
- rephrasing in order to express the student's ideas more clearly and precisely
- guiding the student towards a more economical use of language, so twenty words aren't used when five would be better

7

**PART TWO:
Pairwork**

Activities in this section have been designed for two people working together. They can be used in a one-to-one lesson with the teacher and student each taking roles or with larger classes as pairwork activities.

Students interested in practising social English and telephoning will find this section particularly relevant and work will involve the appropriacy of language and levels of formality.

**PART THREE:
Group work**

Activities in this section are suitable for small group work though most can be adapted for the one-to-one lesson if the teacher joins in the discussion.

Students who need to participate in meetings and discussions will find the work in this section particularly relevant.

Wherever possible the students perform the tasks as themselves rather than taking on the role of fictitious characters. For example, when negotiating 'A contract of sale' the students are involved in buying and selling the actual products they deal in. Similarly, in discussions the students are expected to give their own views and relate their own past experiences.

Self study

Learning English should be seen as a process that will continue for a long period. To equip students with some of the study skills they will need, there are self study tasks in grey boxes throughout the text. Teachers might like to set them as homework or work on them in class. There are also ideas for continuing with English studies on page 111.

Needs analysis

1 What does the company you work for do?

2 What is your job?

3 What are your responsibilities?

4 In which areas of English do you want most practice?

- [ ] speaking
- [ ] listening
- [ ] reading
- [ ] writing
- [ ] grammar
- [ ] vocabulary

5 What do you need to do in English?

- [ ] Give presentations. — Who do you give them to?
  What are they about?
- [ ] Negotiate. — What about?
  Who with?
- [ ] Make phone calls. — Who to?
  What about?
- [ ] Write letters/telexes reports etc. — What about?
- [ ] Show visitors around your place of work. — Who are the visitors?
  What are they interested in seeing?
- [ ] Take part in meetings and discussions. — What about?
- [ ] Describe technical machinery or processes. — What?
- [ ] Explain figures/graphs etc. — What are they about?
- [ ] Socialize with clients. — Where?
- [ ] Anything else? — What?

6 What areas do you feel weakest in and what are your priorities for study on this course?

7 Have you ever studied English before?
Where and for how long?

8 How do you intend to continue with your studies after this course?

Student's notes

Welcome to IN AT THE DEEP END. This book has been designed to help you talk about the subjects you are interested in. You can select activities closely related to your work and express your own ideas and opinions in the lesson. Look through the activities and tell your teacher which ones you think will be most useful to you.

Use English when you speak to your teacher and other students. Here are some expressions that will be useful:

PART ONE: ONE-TO-ONE

1 Survival English

You're phoning someone in England. It's a bad line and they can't hear you very well. They ask you to spell:
- your name
- your company's name
- your address

Then they ask you for your telephone numbers (home and work).

Alphabet pronunciation

1 Which letters rhyme with **A**?
2 Which letters rhyme with **B**?
3 Which letters start with the sound /e/? *eg* F
You can check your answers on page 112.

These letters are commonly confused. Make sure you know them.
A E G H I J Q R U Y

Spell the names on these business cards:

David Csernovicz

QUICK REPLY LTD

The Jupiter Building
96/98 West Road
Leighton Buzzard
Bedfordshire LU7 3BJ
Tel: (0734) 372245
Telex: QUP 49806

Elfrida Heath

CLAC courses

10 Shelford Park Avenue
Great Shelford
Cambridge
CB2 5LU
Tel: 0223 844101 (24 hour answering service)
Telex: 817936 CAMTEL

Highland Enterprises

242 Duke Street
Edinburgh EB7 24Y
Tel: 031 246 8071
Telex: 437961

Moya Lonsdale
Sales Representative

Someone is querying some invoices. Give them the information on the list below.

eg Invoice number thirteen, dated December the seventeenth nineteen eighty seven, is for five hundred and twenty six pounds, seventeen pence.

Invoice No.	Date	Amount
013	December 17th 1987	£526.17
106	12th July 1988	£214.95
119	Aug. 30th 1988	$1,387.86
141	16.11.88	DM 25.50
286	21st Feb. 1989	£2,406.05

Word stress

Note where the main stress falls in these numbers when they are used on their own.

13   thirteen   30   thirty   36   thirty six

But notice what happens when they are followed by another word.

thirteen books   thirteen per cent

3 Time

1 What time do banks open and close in your country?
2 And what about shops, pubs and offices?

"Excuse me, could you tell me what time you open?"

3 Say when these flights depart.

eg flight LH8821 leaves at ten thirty

DEPARTURES		
BA 7530	09:50	PARIS
AE 2943	10:15	STUTTGART
LH 8821	10:30	MILAN
BR 8778	10:50	MOSCOW
DM 0261	11:05	ISTANBUL

4 Mathematics

Read these sums out:

eg $2 + 2 \div 2 \times 2 - 2 = 2$

   Two plus two divided by two times two minus two equals two.

$12 + 6 \div 9 \times 10 - 2 = 18$

$\frac{3}{4} + \frac{1}{2} - \frac{2}{3} = \frac{7}{12}$

$\sqrt{64} \times 3^3 = 72$

$4{\cdot}12 \div 2 = 2.06$

$75 + 15\% = 86.25$

You can check your answers on page 112.

... the average British family has 2.4 children

2 Jobs and responsibilities

1 Organization structure

1 Draw an organization chart for your company, then explain your company's structure.
2 Describe the organization of the different departments.
3 Say what people do and who they are responsible to.
4 Be prepared to answer questions about:
- which departments perform well/badly
- which departments work the hardest
- where communications are good/poor
- which other parts of the organization your department has close links with

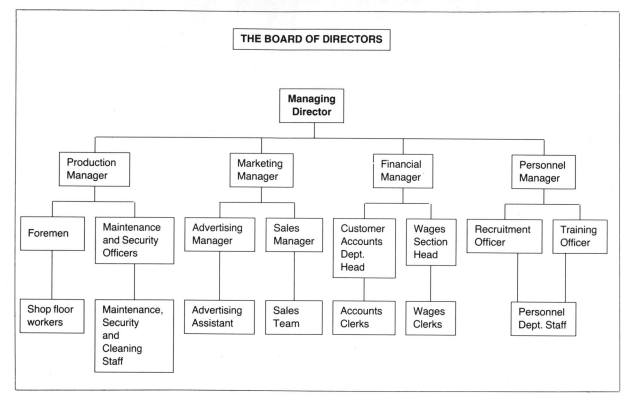

Responsibility
► . . . is responsible for the day to day running of . . .
► . . . is in charge of the Accounts Department.
► . . . runs the agency in Paris.

Job
► . . . deals with new customers.
► . . . looks after the machinery.
► . . . takes care of special accounts.
► . . . sees to repairs.

Position
► Over him there are . . .
► There are . . . under her.
► He reports to . . .
► She is responsible to . . .

2 Time management

Think about your typical working day.

1 How long do you spend:
- talking to people?
- on the phone?
- working on your own?
- working with a computer?
- travelling?

► a lot of	time		
► not much			
► around	half my time		
► about			
► less than	an hour	a	day
► more than	two hours		week

2 How often do you:
- work overtime?
- use English at work?
- travel abroad on business?
- entertain customers?
- have a holiday?

► every		day
► once	a	week
► twice		fortnight
► three times		month
		year

3 What time do you start work in the mornings?
4 And when do you finish?
5 How do you get to work?
6 How long does it take?
7 What do you do to relax in the evenings?

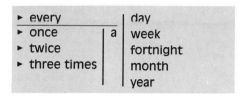

always
usually
sometimes   frequency
not often
hardly ever
never

3 Advantages and disadvantages

1 What are the advantages and disadvantages of your job? Give your job a score from 0 (very bad) to 5 (very good) on the chart below.

	score (0–5)
interesting work	
length of holidays	
flexibility of working hours	
salary or wages	
fringe benefits	
job security	
level of stress	
level of job satisfaction	
level of control over the work organization	
pleasant working environment	
relationships with colleagues	

2 Which of the factors above are most important for you?

3 What qualities do you need to do your job successfully?

4 What information would you include in an advert for your job?

£30,291 – £32,106 p.a

We require a qualified solicitor with at least five years' experience, highly developed management skills and the ability to lead a professional team. Acting as deputy to the Director, you will control the work of the corporate law department.

ARE YOU TIRED OF BEING A SMALL COG IN A BIG MACHINE?

Can you take initiative and work well under pressure? We need a dynamic young Sound Engineer to assist the Production Manager in a fast expanding sonic alarm company. Top salary, company pension scheme and car for right applicant.

PART TIME PACKER

To work in the despatch department of busy, friendly sportswear company. Full training given. 20 hours per week. Good benefits, including 6 weeks holiday p.a. and luncheon vouchers.

► One good thing about my job is . . .

► Another is . . .

► The bad thing about it is . . .

► I like . . .

► I don't like . . .

► I'd like . . .

► I wouldn't like . . .

4 Job definition

Outline your job definition. Make rough notes first, using the form below. The example on page 19 may help you. Explain:

- what you are responsible for
- how your performance is measured
- where you have the authority to change things

JOB DEFINITION	
JOB TITLE:	Pastry Department Manager
COMPANY/BRANCH/DEPT:	Orts the Bakers
RESPONSIBLE TO:	The Bakery Manager
MAIN PURPOSE:	To supervise and control the activities of the Pastry Dept. in order to achieve sales and profit targets.

ANSWERABLE FOR	MEASURE OF PERFORMANCE
Staff Train Staff for the Pastry Dept. Organize and supervise the activities of the Pastry Dept. staff.	Ability of staff to do job. Cost of staff. Staff turnover.
Cleanliness, hygiene and safety Ensure that standards of cleanliness and hygiene meet the Manager's requirement. Maintain Bakery packaging equipment in efficient, safe and hygienic condition.	No deviation from Company standards or statutory requirements.
Merchandise Keep shops stocked with a full range of goods. Ensure that packages are clearly marked with the correct weight and price. Meet sales targets. Maintain adequate stock levels without waste.	Lines out of stock. Customer complaints. Pricing and packaging errors. Wastage %. Sales volume. Gross profit %.
Regulations Ensure observation of all regulations relating to the sale of foodstuffs and safety of equipment.	Reported breaches of regulations.
Authority To vary the 'mix' of goods produced.	

Self study: Easily confused words

Make a list of the words you used to outline your job definition, e.g. check, control, organize, supervise, maintain, repair. Make sure you know the difference between words with similar meanings. A good dictionary will help you.

These words are often confused. Do you know how to use them?

check/control	financial/economic	raise/rise
deliver/despatch	say/tell	advertise/announce
enquire/query	maintain/repair	safety/security
training/education	lend/borrow	notice/note
miss/lose	remember/remind	

3 Instructions

1 Operating machines

Explain how to use:
- a public telephone
- the photocopier at work
- the automatic cash dispenser at your bank
- a video tape recorder

Sequencers
- First (ly) . . .
- Then . . .
- Next . . .
- After that . . .
- Finally . . .

Instructions
- You have to . . . (it's necessary)
- You mustn't . . . (it's wrong)
- You needn't . . . (it's not necessary)
- You don't have to . . . (it's not necessary)

2 Job instructions

Think of a job you do regularly at work. Explain how to do it to a new member of staff. Explain why it has to be done in a particular way.

General truths
- If you press this key, the computer prints out the reading.
- If you open the door, the power is automatically cut off.

  IF + DOES , DO

Warnings
- If you press this key by mistake, you'll lose all the data.
- If you don't inform the accounts department, we won't get paid.

  IF + DOES , WILL DO

3 Games rules

Think of a game you know well (*eg* football, chess, poker) and explain the rules.

4 Directions

1 Draw a rough plan of the building you work in. Give directions for getting from one place to another.

2 An English client is coming to visit your place of work. Tell him/her how to get there from the airport.

► Go along	until you come to . . .		
► Go straight on			
► Turn	left right	at the	end of the corridor roundabout
		when you get to . . .	
► Take the	first second	turning on the	right left
► Follow the signs to . . .			
► Come off the motorway at . . .			

4 Processes

1 Complaints

1 Describe the sort of complaints you have to deal with and make in your job.
2 Give an account of an occasion on which you dealt with/made a complaint.
3 Describe the mechanism or process your company has for dealing with complaints.

> I'd like to make a complaint. It concerns that duck egg you sold me.

Self study: Make and do

Some nouns are used with the verb 'make'
eg He made a complaint.

Some nouns are used with the verb 'do'.
eg She did something about it.

Decide whether these nouns are used with **make** or **do** and put them in the appropriate box. The example sentences in a good dictionary can help you. You can check your answers on page 112.

a profit	work	a telephone call
enquiries	a favour	money
a discovery	a journey	business
a loss	a mistake	one's best
a decision	a joke	a suggestion
an offer	love	excuses
damage	friends	a choice

Make	**Do**

Make is often used if the action is creative.
eg He made a boat in his spare time.

Do is often used if the action is a job or a task. The action needn't be stated.
eg I'll do it.

If you're not sure whether to use **do** or **make**, use **make**. You're more likely to be right!

2 The mouse trap

Label the machine and then describe how it works.

You can check your answers on page 112.

- ► piece of cheese
- ► crane
- ► boxing glove
- ► pulley
- ► conveyor belt
- ► boot
- ► cage

- ► to kick into
- ► to lift up
- ► to punch onto
- ► to carry along
- ► to drop into
- ► to pick up
- ► to eat

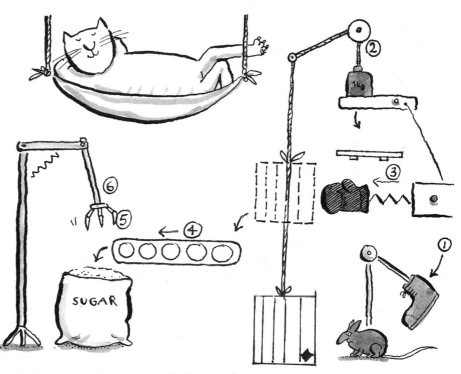

3 Flow charts

Think of a process in your work place such as:

- a production process
- a staff recruitment process
- wage negotiations
- grievance procedures
- communications procedures
- an ordering process
- a staff training process
- a product development process

1 Draw a flow chart showing the different *steps and *stages in the process.
2 Describe the process, explaining clearly the order of events.
3 Explain why things are done in the way they are.

* a step = one action in a process.

* a stage = a series of actions which form part of a process.

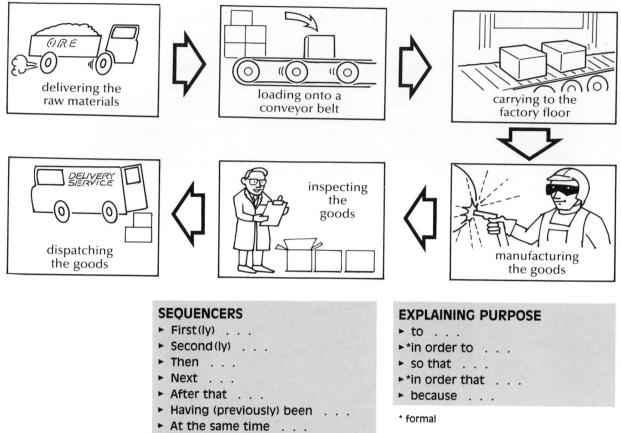

delivering the raw materials

loading onto a conveyor belt

carrying to the factory floor

manufacturing the goods

inspecting the goods

dispatching the goods

SEQUENCERS

- First(ly) . . .
- Second(ly) . . .
- Then . . .
- Next . . .
- After that . . .
- Having (previously) been . . .
- At the same time . . .
- Simultaneously . . .
- Lastly . . .
- Finally . . .

EXPLAINING PURPOSE

- to . . .
- *in order to . . .
- so that . . .
- *in order that . . .
- because . . .

* formal

5 Machines

1 Shapes

Say the name of these shapes and the adjective that describes them.
eg It's a circle. It's circular or round

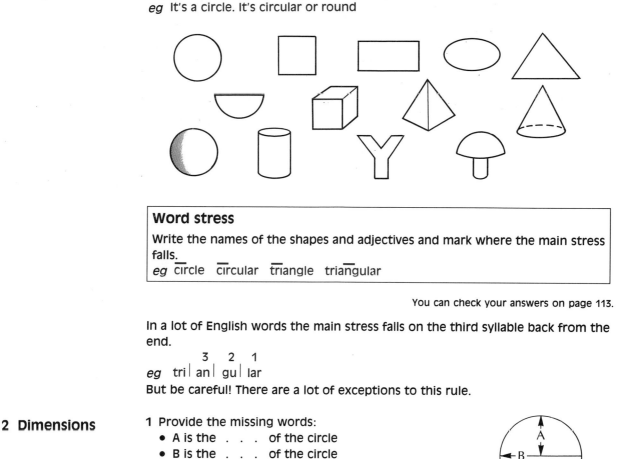

Word stress

Write the names of the shapes and adjectives and mark where the main stress falls.
eg c̄ircle c̄ircular t̄riangle triān̄gular

You can check your answers on page 113.

In a lot of English words the main stress falls on the third syllable back from the end.

       3   2   1
eg tri| an| gu| lar

But be careful! There are a lot of exceptions to this rule.

2 Dimensions

1 Provide the missing words:
  • A is the . . . of the circle
  • B is the . . . of the circle
  • C·is the . . . of the circle
2 Say the dimensions in these diagrams.
  eg The box is 10cm high. The height of the box is 10cm

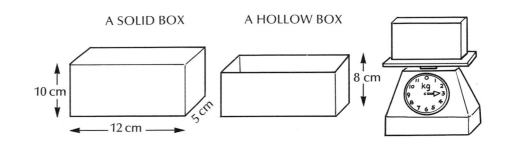

A SOLID BOX   A HOLLOW BOX

10 cm

12 cm   5 cm   8 cm

3 Provide the missing words:
- the box is 2 . . . 4 . . . 3 metres
- the cubic capacity is . . .
- it has a cubic capacity of . . .
- the base is . . . square metres

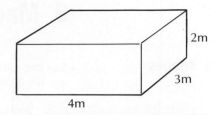

You can check your answers on page 113.

3 Simple objects

What are you carrying about with you in your pockets? Find something interesting and describe it (if your pockets are empty, choose one of the objects below instead):

- define it

- describe its composition

- say what it's made of

- describe its shape and dimensions

- describe the location of the parts

▸ . . . a tool/a thing/an instrument/a device
▸ It's a device for . . . (–ing)
▸ It consists of . . .
▸ It's made up of . . .
▸ It's composed of . . .
▸ . . . a metal blade . . .
▸ . . . made of plastic . . .
▸ . . . a rectangular box
▸ . . . a conical hole about 1cm in diameter.
▸ The battery is housed in a plastic case.
▸ The blade is secured to the top of the box by a screw.

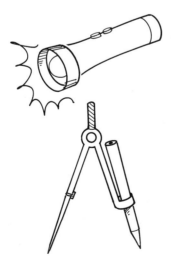

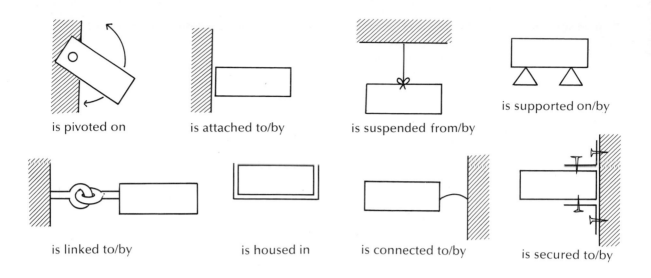

is pivoted on   is attached to/by   is suspended from/by   is supported on/by

is linked to/by   is housed in   is connected to/by   is secured to/by

How many of these words can you use to describe the mouse trap on page 23?

4 Scientific devices

Choose one of the objects below and:
- define it
- describe it
- say how it works

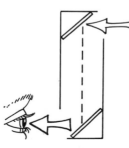

A PERISCOPE   A THERMOMETER   AN ELECTRIC CIRCUIT

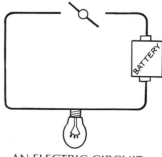

5 A machine

Describe a machine in your work place. Include information about:
- what it's for
- its general composition
- its shape, dimensions and what it's made of
- how it works

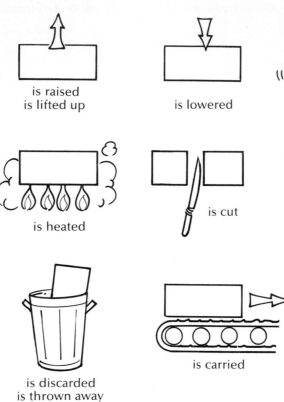

is raised
is lifted up

is lowered

is dropped

is heated

is cut

is controlled

is discarded
is thrown away

is carried

is turned

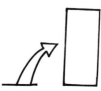

is painted

is rotated

is dipped

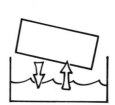

is weighed

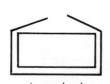

is packed

is transported

6 Systems

1 Taxation

1 Give an outline of the tax system in your country.
2 Explain how direct taxes (eg income tax) are calculated and collected.
3 Explain how indirect taxes (eg VAT) are calculated and collected.
4 What things qualify for tax relief or allowances (eg interest on loans for home purchases)?
5 How are local taxes collected and used?
6 How would you like to change the tax system?

Presenting information

Classifying

► There are two | types of . . .
              | kinds of . . .
              | sorts of . . .
► . . . can be divided into three | types
                              | categories
► . . . comes into the first category

Giving examples

► For example . . .
► Take . . . for instance
► . . . such as . . .

Direct and indirect taxation

2 The sale of alcohol

1 Describe the laws surrounding the sale of alcohol in your country. Explain:
  • where it can be bought
  • age restrictions
  • time restrictions
  • advertising restrictions
  • how it's taxed
2 How would you like to change the laws?

3 Complex systems

Choose a complex social system, such as your country's political, educational or legal system, and describe how it operates. Make notes first, planning the ground you are going to cover in your talk. You might like to suggest ways in which the system could be improved.

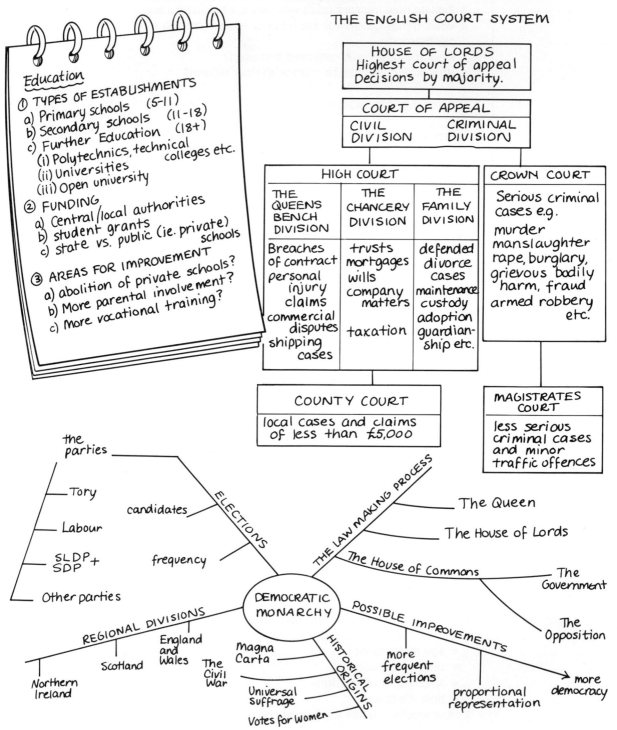

Education

① TYPES OF ESTABLISHMENTS
  a) Primary schools (5-11)
  b) Secondary schools (11-18)
  c) Further Education (18+)
    (i) Polytechnics, technical colleges etc.
    (ii) Universities
    (iii) Open university

② FUNDING
  a) Central/local authorities
  b) student grants
  c) state vs. public (ie. private) schools

③ AREAS FOR IMPROVEMENT
  a) abolition of private schools?
  b) More parental involvement?
  c) More vocational training?

THE ENGLISH COURT SYSTEM

HOUSE OF LORDS
Highest court of appeal
Decisions by majority.

COURT OF APPEAL
CIVIL DIVISION — CRIMINAL DIVISION

HIGH COURT

THE QUEENS BENCH DIVISION	THE CHANCERY DIVISION	THE FAMILY DIVISION
Breaches of contract personal injury claims commercial disputes shipping cases	trusts mortgages wills company matters taxation	defended divorce cases maintenance custody adoption guardianship etc.

CROWN COURT
Serious criminal cases e.g. murder manslaughter rape, burglary, grievous bodily harm, fraud armed robbery etc.

COUNTY COURT
local cases and claims of less than £5,000

MAGISTRATES COURT
less serious criminal cases and minor traffic offences

DEMOCRATIC MONARCHY

the parties
— Tory
— Labour
— SLDP + SDP
— Other parties

ELECTIONS
candidates
frequency

THE LAW MAKING PROCESS
— The Queen
— The House of Lords
— The House of Commons
— The Government
— The Opposition

REGIONAL DIVISIONS
Northern Ireland
Scotland
England and Wales

HISTORICAL ORIGINS
Magna Carta
The Civil War
Universal Suffrage
Votes for Women

POSSIBLE IMPROVEMENTS
more frequent elections
proportional representation
more democracy

Introducing the topic	Mapping the talk
▸ I'm going to | talk about . . . explain . . . outline . . . describe . . .	▸ I'll start with . . . ▸ Then I'll go on to . . . ▸ I'll also . . . ▸ Finally . . .

4 Company systems

You are responsible for the induction of a new worker in your company/department. Explain the system for:

- remuneration (pay)
- hours of work/overtime
- the pension scheme
- sickness
- holidays
- tea breaks and lunch arrangements
- cloakroom facilities
- smoking
- first aid
- car parking
- staff discounts

7 Descriptions

1 Places

Describe your country and home town.

<table>
<tr><td>

Country

Population:

Industry:

Natural resources:

Agriculture:

Climate:

Religion:

Politics:

</td><td>

Town

Population:

Situation: (north, south, east, west, etc.)

Historic buildings:

Main industries:

Leisure facilities:

</td></tr>
</table>

"Describe your country."

Self study: dictionary skills

Uncountable nouns such as scenery, oil and snow can't be plural. Notice the difference this makes in the sentence below.

There's a lot of nice scenery.
There are a lot of farms.

There isn't much snow.
There aren't many towns.

There isn't any oil.
There aren't any mountains.

Decide whether these nouns are countable or uncountable and put them in the appropriate box. You can get the information you need from a good learner's dictionary. Look for **C** (countable) or **U** (uncountable) after the words.

research	work	advice
machine	traffic	pound (£)
money	chair	experiment
equipment	suggestion	information
car	machinery	fact
furniture	job	

Countable	Uncountable

Answers on page 113

2 Brainstorming adjectives

1 Think of as many words as you can that could be used to describe:
  • the weather
  • the building you work in
  • beer
  • a book
  • your boss
  • your husband/wife
  • your company's image
2 Make a list of the adjectives you used. Think of adjectives with opposite meanings to the ones you have collected. Use prefixes like un–, in–, im–, ir–, dis–, and non–, to help you.

3 Look at the lists of adjectives you have collected.
How many adjectives can be turned into nouns?
eg spacious → space
    comfortable → comfort

3 Selling

1 Choose an object in the classroom and 'sell' it to your teacher.
Touch it, feel it, etc. and use adjectives with positive overtones to describe it.
Explain its purpose and value. What special or unusual qualities does it have?
2 Now do the same for one of your products. What information would you
include in an advertisement for the product?

Self study: Catalogues and brochures

Go through an English catalogue for the products or services your company
sells. Highlight or underline all the adjectives you find. Which ones do you find
interesting and think you could use? Make a note of the sentences they
appear in.

---

4 Product range

Give a presentation of the range of products or services your company offers.
Divide the products into different categories. Classify them according to their
use and purpose, the materials they are made of, how they are made, who they
are sold to, etc.

The range

▶ We have a wide *range of . . .
▶ This *line is at the top/bottom of the range.
▶ . . . come in different styles/colours/sizes, etc.

---

* range = the different products your company sells

* line = a particular product

Use and purpose

▶ It's used for . . .
▶ It's used as . . .
▶ It's suitable for . . .

Selling the product

▶ It sells well in . . .
▶ It's popular with . . .
▶ It costs . . .
▶ It retails at £3.50

Comparing products

▶ It's a kind of . . .
▶ It's similar to . . .
▶ It's an alternative to . . .
▶ It's a version of . .

Construction

▶ It's made of . . .
▶ It consists of . . .
▶ It's made up of . . .

8 Comparisons

1 Better and best

1 Compare
- an abacus with a pocket calculator
- your car with your teacher's car
- two different ways of investing money

2 Consider the points below, then give your opinion. Say which you think is better.

Calculating machines	Cars	Investments
size	size	risk
speed	age	size of investment
weight	price	rate of return
portability	power	tax
efficiency	running costs	accessibility of funds
ease of use	comfort	term
age	boot size	
reliability	engine size	
	speed	
	acceleration	

3 Compare:
- three different forms of transport
- three different jobs
- your country with two other countries

4 Consider the points below, then give your opinion. Say which you think is best.

Transport	Jobs	Countries
price	interest	size
speed	stress	population
comfort	difficulty	climate
interest	hours of work	scenery
excitement	pay	standard of living
noise	satisfaction	culture
convenience	power and status	food
	training	

First and second class mail

Comparing two things	Comparing three or more things
X is . . . –er than Y.	X is the . . . –est.
X is more . . . than Y.	X is the most . . .
X is less . . . than Y.	X is the least . . .
X isn't as . . . as Y.	

2 Blowing your own trumpet

1 Explain what's so good about:
  • your department
  • your company
  • your products
2 Say what your main strengths and achievements are.
3 What have you got that makes you better than your competitors?

> Team spirit <

3 Company size

1 Do you work in a large or small company?
2 Would you prefer to work in a larger or smaller company? Why?
3 How does size affect the operation of a business concern?
4 Consider the ability of large and small organizations:
- to develop a company spirit
- to offer employees opportunities for promotion
- to provide variety in work tasks
- to operate good communication systems
- to stay in close contact with their customers
- to adapt quickly to changes in the market place
- to spend money on research and development
- to buy materials in bulk

Opportunities

- ▶ There's more opportunity for . . .
- ▶ There are more chances of . . .
- ▶ There's more scope for . . .
- ▶ Large companies can . . .
- ▶ Small companies are able to . . .

Restrictions

- ▶ There's less opportunity for . . .
- ▶ There are fewer chances of . . .
- ▶ There's less scope for . . .
- ▶ Large companies need to . . .
- ▶ Small companies have to . . .

Adding emphasis

▶ Large ▶ Small	companies are	much far somewhat slightly a bit	slower to adapt.

9 Past time

1 Earlier this year

1 Get out your diary and talk about some of the things you did earlier this year. Make a list of the verbs you used. Which are regular and which are irregular?

2 With regular verbs, there are three ways of pronouncing the '–ed' ending in the past tense.

/d/ *eg* phoned, employed
/t/ *eg* worked, produced
/id/ *eg* started, expanded

Decide which sounds the verbs on your list end with.

Regular verbs that end with /d/ or /t/ sound, (eg start, expand) end with the long /id/ sound in the past tense.

2 The last time

When did you last:
- have a holiday?
- speak English at work?
- go out for a meal?
- travel on business?
- sing?
- take a photograph?
- get angry with someone?
- give someone a present?

Time phrases

▶ last	night
	week
	year

▶ yesterday	morning
	afternoon
	evening

▶ two days	ago
▶ a month	
▶ an hour	

Prepositions

| ▶ in | January | (month) |
| | 1987 | (year) |

| ▶ on | April 25th | (date) |
| | Friday | (day) |

| ▶ at | 3 o'clock | (time) |

3 Company history

Give a brief account of your company's history. Say when it was founded and outline some of the main events in the past.

Active voice / Passive voice

▶ Jane Carne founded the company in 1985.
The company was founded in 1985.

▶ The Board made Michael Davis General Manager.
Michael Davis was made General Manager.

4 Anecdotes

Prepare to describe something funny or dangerous that happened:
- in your work place
- while you were travelling
- at a party you went to
- while you were on holiday
- at a sports event you were watching or taking part in

Self study: jokes

What jokes do you know in your own language? Can you tell them in English?
Try recording some onto a cassette for your teacher. If you make mistakes,
record over it again until it's perfect.

---

5 Have you ever . . . ?

Have you ever:
- had your photograph in the newspaper?
- broken something valuable?
- put in an insurance claim?
- forgotten your front door key?
- been on a camping holiday?
- bought something at an auction?
- been stopped by the police?
- won a trophy at a sporting event?
- won a competition?

▸ Have you ever . . . ?
▸ Yes, I have.
▸ No, I haven't.

▸ When was that?
▸ What happened?
▸ Why/Who/Where/How . . . ? etc.

6 Curriculum vitae

Fill in the CV on the following page in note form, then give an account of your career history to date. Be prepared to explain why you did the things you did.

Finished or continuing actions

I worked for Hendersons for two years. (I don't work for Hendersons any more.)
I've worked for Jacobs for two years. (I still work for Jacobs.)

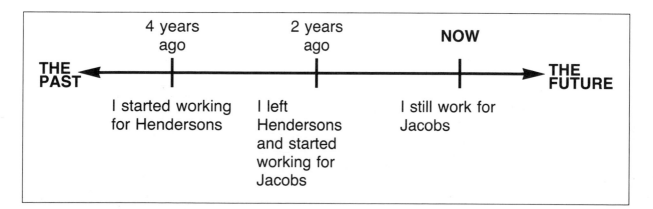

CURRICULUM VITAE   Name:

Date of birth: Address:
Marital status:

Education: Qualifications:
                                        Languages:

Working Experience:

Company	Dates	Position	Responsibilities	Reason for leaving

10 Recent time

1 Giving news

Make notes of some of the changes that have taken place in your company in recent years on the chart below.

Equipment new machinery computer installations
Products new lines introduced old lines scrapped product modifications
The building new premises/extensions alterations refurbishments
Personnel employees who have joined the company employees who have left promotions
Systems company policies changed methods of doing things

You meet someone who used to work for your company several years ago. Tell them about the changes that have taken place since they left.

eg Emma Wood has been promoted to Financial Manager.
    Oh, that's good. When was that?
    Two months ago. And we've altered the design department.
    Really? What did you do to it?

Definite and indefinite time

The present perfect tense is used to give someone news of a past action.
eg We've introduced a new line.
    Adrian's been sacked.

But the past simple tense is used if a definite time is referred to or understood.
eg We launched a new product in January.
    Why was he sacked?

41

Self study: good news, bad news

Tune in to the BBC World Service radio broadcasts and record the news programmes. The first time you listen, play the tape right through without stopping. Don't worry if you miss a lot of words, just listen for the general meaning. Decide what the news items are about.

Pick the news items you are most interested in and play them again. Can you catch the details? Try to pick out:
- specific information
  eg country and place names, people's names, times and dates.
- unfamiliar words:
  guess how they are spelt and look them up in a good English dictionary.

2 The job list

You have to go away on business for a month. Who will do your job while you're away?
1 Write a list of the jobs you want done in your absence.
2 Phone your stand-in after two weeks and find out how they're getting on.
3 Find out which jobs they have done and which jobs they haven't done yet.
   eg Have you ordered the plants yet?
      Yes, I have.
      Good, and have you replaced the light fittings in the boiler room?
      I'm afraid I haven't had time, but I'll do it this week.

MEMO

TO: Simon Barnes   FROM: Michael Black
DATE: 15th April   RE: My absence

I will be in Malaysia for four weeks from 5th March. In emergencies
I can be contacted at The Durban Palace Hotel, 1092 Buta Jampang,
Kuala Lumpur.
While I'm away could you:

1 Get in three quotations for the removal of the hedge at the back of
   the car park. *Quotes received from Maple Homes Ltd and Garden Services.*
                      No quote received from Green Spaces Ltd yet.

2 Order flowering plants for the beds outside the main entrance and
   plant them on arrival. *✓*

3 Make enquiries into the complaint about the dirty stockroom on the
   third floor. *✓ One of the stockmen was locking it each day so the cleaners*
                couldn't get in. Asked him to leave it unlocked.

4 Replace old light fittings in the boiler room with fluorescent
   strip lighting.

5 Check the Night Security staff holiday applications. (Mrs Irvine
   and Mr Skinner have both asked for the first half of August,
   which isn't feasible.) *✓ Mr Skinner now going in September.*

6 Arrange for Iris Stokes (office cleaner) to receive a bunch of
   flowers on the 25th anniversary of her employment here.
   We had the dates wrong. She's only been here 24 years.

7 Put up the new pictures in the entrance lobby.

Thanks for all your help, Simon.

3 Recent actions

Your boss asks you to give an account of the work you have been doing over the
past few weeks. Tell him. Also, explain what you haven't done yet and why.

Completed and uncompleted actions

▶ I've been writing the report (the report may or may not be finished)
▶ I've written the report (the report is finished)
▶ I haven't written the report yet (the report isn't finished)

4 Work in progress

Think of a scheme at work which is in progress now. For example:
- a new sales campaign
- a building reorganization scheme
- a staff training scheme
- a research and development project
- the company pension scheme
- the computerization of a process
- the merging or separation of departments

1 First, outline the targets or goals of the scheme, i.e. what it hopes to accomplish.

2 Then explain:
- what has been done so far
- what is being done now
- what hasn't been done yet

3 Look ahead to the results. When the scheme has been completed, what will have been done?

eg By the end of next year the Marketing and Sales Departments will have moved to their new building and the basement will have been converted into a recreational area.

BUILDING EXPANSION SCHEME	
AIMS:	• To rationalize the use of space in the building. To provide more space for expanding departments, e.g. Marketing, Sales, Personnel. To reduce the space of the Accounts and Records departments now computerization has reduced staff in these areas. • To increase staff access to computer terminals. • To provide a large hall for meetings, conferences, exhibitions, etc. • To improve the working environment for all employees. • To provide staff sporting and recreational facilities.
2 YEARS AGO	Accounts department moved from the 3rd floor to nearby rented accommodation. 3rd floor redecorated. 36 computer terminals installed.
1 YEAR AGO	Accounts department moved back to 3rd floor. 4th floor (old Records department) converted into a Grand Hall. Construction begun on the new Marketing Department buildings.
NOW	Kitchen being refitted. Modern cooking facilities being installed. Canteen being redecorated. Marketing building still not finished.
NEXT YEAR	Marketing and Sales departments to move from basement to new building. Basement to be gutted and redecorated as staff recreational area. New lifts to be installed.
THE YEAR AFTER NEXT	Multigym to be installed in basement. Staff crêche to open in basement. 1st floor to be redecorated. Ground floor to be gutted and open-plan reception area created.

Active voice/Passive voice

► The builders have redecorated the third floor.
The third floor has been redecorated.

► They haven't installed the lifts yet.
The lifts haven't been installed yet.

11 Describing trends

1 The economy

1 What trends have occurred in recent years in your country's economy?
2 What has happened to:
- the rate of inflation?
- interest rates?
- the GNP (Gross National Product)?
- the rate of unemployment?
3 Use the verbs in the box below to describe the changes.

eg The rate of inflation was increasing until 1987 when it evened out. It
dropped to 5% last year.

Do these verbs indicate an upward (↑) downward (↓) or horizontal (→)
movement?

to fall	to decrease	to slip back
to climb	to drop	to go down
to rise	to improve	to remain stable
to even out	to deteriorate	to increase
to decline	to pick up	to reach a peak
to go up	to hit a low	
to bottom out	to recover	

► Which verbs can be made into nouns?
  eg to fall . . . a fall
      to improve . . . an improvement

You can check your answers on page 113.

2 Company trends

1 Describe changes that have taken place in recent years in your company.
Consider:
- turnover
- profits
- number of employees
- range of products
- raw materials prices
- prices of products
- volume of production
- staff working hours
- anything else?
2 Describe the rate of change.
  eg Turnover has increased rapidly.
      There has been a rapid increase in turnover.
3 Describe the size of change.
  eg Turnover has increased noticeably.
      There has been a noticeable increase in turnover.

There was a ⌐rapid⌐ increase in sales.   Sales rose ⌐rapidly.⌐
              adjective   adverb

> An adjective describes a noun (a thing).
> An adverb describes a verb (an action).

Write the appropriate adverbs for the adjectives below. The first ones have been done for you.

Speed or rate of change	
rapid	rapidly
slow	
sudden	
sharp	
steady	
gradual	
fast	

Size of change	
noticeable	noticeably
substantial	
considerable	
slight	
significant	
dramatic	
negligible	

▶ Decide whether these words indicate a fast, medium or slow change.

▶ Decide whether these words indicate a small, medium or large change.

You can check your answers on page 114.

3 Headlines

UK RECOVERY 'GAINING IN PACE'

Boom time at Rolls Royce

Securitight tops profit forecast at £952,000

Shares drop sharply in slow trading

Dorrington share flotation flops

Cocoa prices slump

Record low for United Plastics

Rowan to cut jobs as losses mount

Restrained upturn for German chemicals

LAWSON'S BUDGET ATTACKED

Abaco reduces costs

but losses persist

STEEL OUTPUT WELL AHEAD OF TARGET

Look at the headlines and decide what stories you think they are about. Is it good news or bad news?
Invent some headlines for news stories about your company.

Self study: newspapers

Prediction

Take an English newspaper and look for an interesting headline. Predict the subject of the article from the headline. Try writing a list of the words you expect to see in the article, then read it and see how many you can find.

Gap filling

Make a copy of an article, scribble over some of the words you find interesting, and put it away for a few days. See if you can remember the missing words when you look at it again.

Jigsaws

Make a copy of a long newspaper article. Cut it up with scissors into paragraphs, then try to reconstruct it. You'll need to look closely at the words used to link ideas. This will improve your understanding of how the information is connected and organized.

Unknown words

It's possible to understand an article without knowing the meaning of lots of the words. Can you guess words efficiently? Before looking a word up in a dictionary, guess and note down what it means and what type of word it is.
eg if it's a thing (noun)
    if it's an action (verb)
    if it's describing something (adjective)
Check your guess in a good dictionary.

4 Explaining a graph

Draw a graph showing trends relevant to your field of work. (Look back to activity 2 for ideas if necessary.) Indicate events that affected the figures on the graph. Then interpret the graph, describing movements and giving reasons for them.

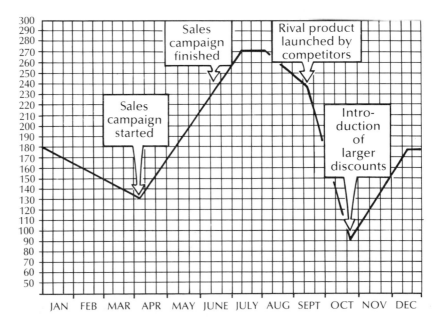

Causes and results

▶ Sales rose steeply in April | as a result of | the spring sales campaign.
owing to
due to
because of

▶ The launching of a rival product | was the reason for | the decline in September.
caused
resulted in
explains

▶ Larger discounts were introduced in October. | That's why | sales picked
Consquently | up in
So | November.

12 Planning ahead

I'm afraid Mrs Hesketh can't see you this morning.

That's all right. I'll come back tomorrow.

Decide how to deal with these problems:
1 'I'm afraid I won't have time to type this letter.'
2 'I'm afraid the photocopier isn't working.'
3 'I'm afraid I can't give you a lift tomorrow.'
4 'I'm afraid the line's engaged.'
5 'I'm afraid I can't find that report.'
6 'I'm afraid there's nothing good on television tonight.'
7 'I'm afraid there's no hot water.'

2 Intentions

1 You're tired, depressed and suffering from executive stress. You have written a list of all your problems and now you're going to decide what to do about them.

eg I'll reorganize the office.

Problems	Solutions
I can never find anything at work	I'll reorganize the office
I'm tired	
I can't get to sleep at night	
I smoke too much	
I'm not fit enough	
I'm overweight	
I'm broke	
The boss is angry with me	
My English isn't good enough	

2 Now you've decided what to do you feel much better. Tell your colleague what you intend doing.

eg I can never find anything at work, so I'm going to reorganize.

3 What problems are you facing at work at the moment?
What are you going to do about them?

▸ I'm going to . . .
▸ We're planning to . . .
▸ I'm intending to . . .
▸ We're hoping to . . .

▸ Which of these forms sounds less definite?

3 Fixed plans and arrangements

Take out your diary and say what you're doing in the next few weeks.
eg I'm visiting the new factory site on Monday.

(If you haven't got your diary with you, use the one below, but be careful: it's written in note form so some words are missing.)

MONDAY	10 a.m. Visit new factory site and Mr Fairview (builder) 3 p.m. Interview Caroline Laidlaw for new sales job.
TUESDAY	11.30 a.m. Tax office. Meeting with Mr Grabbit (tax inspector) 8 p.m. Maggie's cocktail party at No 10.
WEDNESDAY	9 a.m. Marketing Dept. meeting Agenda: 1990s campaign. 8 p.m. Guest speaker at Geographical Society dinner.
THURSDAY	9.30 a.m. Appointment with Mrs. Olsen - Swedish Embassy. 1pm. Lunch at Mange Tout restaurant + wife.
FRIDAY	10.55 am. Fly to New York Marketing conference.

List.
Go to b
Haird
Pack
Don't
to po

That's funny. I'm having a holiday there in sixteen years' time too.

4 Changes of plan

Of course things don't always run according to plan. Make some changes to your schedule and alter the diary. Say what you were going to do and what the new plans are.
eg I was going to visit the new factory site on Monday but now I'm taking the day off.
I wasn't going to go to Newcastle, but now I am.

13 Future possibilities

1 Contingency plans

You're making a very important speech at a conference tomorrow. You can't afford to let anything go wrong, so you have to plan for all eventualities. What will you do if:

- you are too nervous to sleep tonight?
- you go home and discover your best suit is at the cleaners?
- you lose your notes?
- your car breaks down on the way?
- you break your glasses?
- you lose your voice?

The first conditional

▶ If I feel too nervous to sleep, I'll pour myself a large whisky.
▶ If I still don't sleep after that, at least I won't be worried anymore.

IF　+　DOES ,　　　　　　WILL　DO

2 Planning your manpower

Consider the manpower in your department now. How will it be affected by changes in the future?

First consider the present situation:

1 Do you have the right number of staff? Are they employed in the right places? | Is anyone over- or under-worked? Are the numbers sufficient to maintain coverage in an emergency?

2 Do the jobs match the capabilities of each person? | Do you operate a staff appraisal system? How are staff selected and trained for promotion?

Then consider your possible future needs:

3 Is any expansion or contraction likely? | Will this require more staff/different skills/less staff?

4 Is any increase in trade likely? | Will this require more staff, part time, full time or seasonally?

3 Will conditions of work alter? | Will staffing requirements be affected by changes in hours of work/length and timing of holidays/overtime policies/productivity, etc?

6 Will there be any changes in products/systems/methods? | Will this necessitate new skills/ retraining, etc?

► We'll need more staff	if when in case	trade increases.
► We won't need more staff	until/till unless	

► What are the differences in meaning between the sentences above?

You can check your answers on page 114.

3 Company forecast

1 Forecast your company's future.
How will it be affected by:
  • modern technological advances?
  • present management strategies?
  • changes in government policy?
  • external economic factors?
     eg changes in interest rates/recession/economic growth/inflation
Say what you think will happen to:
  • demand for your products
  • your production methods and costs
  • the labour/employment situation in your industry

Giving opinions
► I expect . . .
► I feel confident that . . .
► I doubt if . . .
►*I reckon . . .
► I don't doubt that . . .
► I'd be surprised if . . .
►*I wouldn't mind betting . . .

► Which phrases suggest the speaker:
  a is sure something will happen?
  b thinks it's likely?
  c thinks it's unlikely?

* informal

Answers on page 114.

4 Degress of certainty

Decide how certain the speaker is in these sentences and match each one to the appropriate picture. Pick out the words that helped you decide the level of certainty and note them in the boxes.

1 Demand for our products isn't likely to decrease.
2 The war in the Middle East might affect raw material supplies.
3 There won't be a recovery in our balance of payments.
4 The dollar is bound to increase in value.
5 Interest rates will probably remain steady.
6 There's no chance of the government reducing taxation.
7 It's likely that wages will rise faster than inflation.
8 Many small companies could go bankrupt.
9 Finding skilled staff probably won't be a problem.
10 There'll be a lot of technological advances in this field.

Answers on page 115.

Definite	
Likely	
Possible	
Unlikely	
Definitely not	

5 Project planning

Plan a new research and development project in your workplace. Describe how it could be organized with reference to:
• the aims and goals of the project
• staffing
• space
• equipment
• time
• cost and funding

14 Hypothesizing

1 Stating preference

Would you prefer to:
- have longer holidays or a higher salary?
- have your job or your boss's job?
- live in a large house a long way from your work or live in a small flat within walking distance?
- have a butler or a chauffeur?
- be a brilliant painter or a brilliant novelist?
- have a holiday house or a yacht?
- have a male or a female boss?

> ▸ I'd prefer . . . (to do)
> ▸ I'd rather . . . (do)

2 Supposing

1 Supposing you could have a large sum of money to invest in your department or company, what would you do with it? What would you try to improve?
2 Supposing you could reorganize the television broadcasting service in your country, what would you do? What changes would you make?
3 Supposing you could decide how much tax to charge on a packet of cigarettes, what would you do? Why?
4 Supposing you were offered another job at twice your present salary but in another country, would you take it? What would you need to consider?
5 Supposing you were ten years younger than you are now, would you change your life in any way? How?
6 Supposing you were made redundant, what would you do?

> **Stating conditions**
> ▸ It'd depend on . . .
> ▸ I'd have to know . . .
> ▸ I'd have to consider . . .

The second conditional
- ► If I were 10 years younger,
- ► If I could take my family with me,
- ► As long as | it was well paid,
- ► Providing |

      IF   +   DID   ,   WOULD DO

I'd take the job.

3 Unusual circumstances

It's unlikely to happen, but in what situations might you:
- send food back in a restaurant?
- resign?
- go on strike?
- emigrate?
- join the army?
- drive your car after you had been drinking?
- dye your hair?
- lie to your English teacher?

- ► I | would | join the army, if there was a war.
-     | might |

► What difference does the use of **would** or **might** make to this sentence?

- ► I'd only go on strike, if | there was no alternative.
- ► I would't go on strike, unless |

    WOULD DO   ,   IF + DID

4 What would you have done?

These things happened to someone else. But what would you have done if they had happened to you?

1 'I noticed a strong smell of smoke coming from the flat below.'

2 'I knew I'd only paid for a tourist class seat so I was very surprised when the air hostess showed me to a first class seat.'

3 'She'd spent a lot of money on the dress but it looked awful, so when she asked me if I liked it . . .'

4 'I gave him a £5 note but he must have thought it was a tenner because he gave me £7.25 change. I didn't realize till after I'd left the shop and I was already late for my appointment.'

5 'My traveller's cheques still hadn't arrived on the day I was due to leave.'

6 'Betty had shown me her plans for the advertising compaign and she trusted me completely so it was very embarrassing when the Managing Director congratulated me on my ideas.'

- ► I'd have . . .
- ► I wouldn't have . . .

5 Things that didn't happen

1 Think back to a time in your life when you've made a decision, or chosen between several alternative courses of action:
- deciding what career to follow
- deciding to take a training course
- deciding to accept a job
- deciding to get married
- deciding where to live

How would your life have been different if you had made a different decision?

2 Think of something that has had a significant effect on your life:
- a trip you've made
- a person you've met
- an interest you've developed
- a book you've read

How would your life have been different if it hadn't happened?

The third conditional
▶ If I'd turned this job down, I'd have regretted it for the rest of my life.
▶ If I hadn't gone to that meeting, I wouldn't have met my wife.

IF   +   HAD DONE   ,   WOULD HAVE DONE

15 Presentations

1 Public speaking

1 You are chairing a conference. Make a speech of welcome on the first morning.
2 You are a guest speaker at an English Rotary Club lunch. Introduce yourself and say a little about Rotary Club activities in your country.
3 Introduce the guest speaker at your company's annual dinner and dance, then thank him/her at the end.
4 Think of a situation in which you might be called on to speak in public. Explain the situation, then give the speech.

Welcoming
- ▶ Good morning, ladies and gentlemen.
- ▶ Welcome to . . .
- ▶ It's very nice to see you all here today.

Questions
- ▶ If anyone has any questions, please feel free to interrupt.
- ▶ If you have any questions, I'll do my best to answer them (later).

Introducing a speaker
- ▶ Miss Eustace has kindly agreed to come along today to speak to us about . . .
- ▶ Ladies and Gentlemen, Miss Caroline Eustace . . . (clapping)
- ▶ It gives me great pleasure to introduce Miss Caroline Eustace . . . (clapping)

Thanking a speaker
- ▶ On behalf of everyone here, I'd like to thank Miss Eustace for a most interesting and entertaining/ enlightening/informative talk.
- ▶ Thank you very much indeed, Miss Eustace. I'm sure I'm speaking for us all when I say how much we've appreciated your being here today.

Finishing
- ▶ Thank you very much.
- ▶ Thank you for being so attentive.

2 On the spur of the moment

You have just two minutes to prepare before you give a talk on one of these topics:

- how good presentations can benefit your company
- how speakers should prepare before giving presentations
- the qualities of a good speaker
- how a speaker can keep the attention of the audience
- the effective use of visual aids in presentations

3 A prepared presentation

Prepare and make a presentation on a topic of your own choice. For example:

- your company
- your products
- a project you have been involved in recently
- new developments in your field

Before you begin, decide:

- who you are talking to
- how many people there are
- who they are
- if it's a formal or informal occasion

Prepare any props you need, *eg* white board, projector slides, etc. Write brief notes outlining the talk.

Company Presentation Notes
1 Who it was founded by ....
2 Date it was founded ....
3 Nature of business ....
4 The type of customers it has ....
5 Location(s) ....
6 Number of employees ....
7 Annual turnover ....
8 Location of headquarters ....
9 Group turnover ....
10 Number of group employees ....
11 The company's main strength ....
12 The company's future plans ....

4 Questions

Go back over your presentation and think of the questions members of the audience could ask. Ask the questions, then answer them.

Pinpointing the reference

► You mentioned . . .
► Could I go back to the point you made about . . . ?
► I was interested in your comments on . . .
► You said that . . .

Asking for clarification

► Could you say a little more about that?
► Could you expand on that?
► Could you clarify what you said about . . . ?
► I'm still a bit confused about . . .

I obviously didn't explain that clearly enough.

Mm. That's a very interesting question.

I'm glad you raised that point.

I'm afraid I don't know the answer to that one.

Let me put it another way.

I want to say something else on that subject.

You didn't listen properly.

I'll say it again so listen this time.

Why did you have to ask that?

Hold on a minute. I'm thinking of an answer.

5 A visitor to your company

Someone is coming to see you at your place of work. You are responsible for his/her visit. Decide who the visitor is (eg client, supplier).

Before they come:

1 Work out which system, processes, products, etc. the visitor will be most interested in. Decide who they should meet and what parts of the building/factory/site they should see. (Also what they can't see!)

2 Work out an *itinerary for the visit. You might like to draw a plan or map showing where you are going to go.

* An itinerary is a plan for a visit with times, places and people to see.

When they come:

3 Meet the visitor, greet them and explain their itinerary to them.

4 Show them round. When appropriate give short presentations on the company history, the company structure, the factory and offices, machinery and equipment, processes, etc. Introduce the visitor to other personnel.

5 Answer any questions that arise.

6 Say goodbye to your visitor.

PART TWO – PAIRWORK

16 Social chit-chat

1 Introductions

1 Introduce two friends at an informal party.
2 Introduce your husband/wife to your Managing Director at a formal social event.
3 You're at a conference and you have just seen someone you've been wanting to meet for ages. Go up to him/her and introduce yourself.
4 You have an appointment to see Mrs Higgins at 3.30. Introduce yourself to the secretary at the reception desk.
5 You have arranged to pick up a client at the airport and take him to his hotel. You've never met him before so you're not sure what he looks like. You see someone who might be your client. Speak to him.

Informal introductions

▶ Have you met Georgina?
▶ Do you know Georgina? Georgina, this is Tom, a friend of mine from work.
▶ Hello.
▶ Hello, nice to meet you.

Formal introductions

▶ Mr Morey, may I introduce you to my wife Barbara? Barbara, this is Mr Morey.
▶ How do you do?

Introducing yourself

▶ May I introduce myself? I'm June Hesketh of Trumpington Engineering.
▶ I have an appointment to see Mr Wilson at 3.30. My name is Richard Baldwin and I'm from French Waters Ltd.
▶ Excuse me, are you Mr Kenney?

2 Striking up a conversation

It's often difficult to start a conversation with strangers. Think of a comment you could make as an 'opener' in these situations:

1 You're waiting on a platform at the station for your train. An old lady who is also waiting says, 'It's a nice day, isn't it?' What do you say?
2 Now you are on the train travelling to a conference in Blackpool. You notice the tags on the luggage of the man sitting opposite you. He is going to the same hotel as you in Blackpool. Perhaps he's attending the same conference. Speak to him.
3 You're at the conference now, waiting for the first talk to start. You recognize the man sitting in front of you. You're sure you have met him before, but you can't remember where. Speak to him.
4 The first speaker at the conference was very interesting. You enjoyed her talk so much you would like to talk to her about it. You happen to be standing near her at coffee time so you say, . . .
5 You sit down for the conference lunch next to someone you don't know. Start a conversation.

Possible answers can be found on page 115.

3 Getting to know someone

Get to know someone a little better. Find out about:

Their job
COMPANY
PRODUCTS/SERVICES
DEPARTMENT
POSITION AND RESPONSIBILITIES

Their interests
HOBBIES/INTERESTS
SPORTS
FAVOURITE MUSIC
FAVOURITE FOODS
FOOD DISLIKES
FAVOURITE BOOKS
FAVOURITE FILMS
HOLIDAYS

Their family
WIFE/HUSBAND
CHILDREN
BROTHERS
SISTERS

Getting information
► Could you tell me (more) about . . . ?
► What's it like?
► What are they like?
► What . . . ?
► Where . . . ?
► When . . . ?
► How . . . ?
► Why . . . ?

Showing interest:

Words	Sounds
► Yes?	► Mmm
► Really?	► Ah
► Is it?	► Uh huh
► Do you?	► Oh

Pronunciation: intonation

The voice is usually high pitch or rises in pitch to show interest in what someone is saying.

Practise responding to what your partner says without using words. Just use sounds with a rising pitch.

4 Quick replies

For this task you have to reply to different remarks. First work out what the situation is. Then reply quickly.

1 Hello, how are you?
2 Thank you for the beautiful flowers.
3 Have you got a penknife on you?
4 Do you mind if I open a window?
5 How's business?
6 You haven't seen a blue umbrella anywhere around here, have you?
7 Fancy a drink on the way home?
8 Have you got the time?
9 How do you do?
10 George sends you his regards.
11 Could you give me a lift to the bank?
12 How did the meeting go?
13 How do you take your coffee?
14 Right then, I'm off.

Possible answers can be found on pages 115–116.

17 Politely does it

1 Requests

Ask people to do things in the following situations:

1 You want your secretary to work late. (It's her birthday.)
2 You want your colleague to give you a lift into town on his way home.
3 You want your boss to let you go on holiday in August instead of September as previously arranged.
4 You want your colleague to help you carry the photocopier upstairs.
5 Your office staff are in the habit of arriving five minutes late each morning. You want this to stop.
6 In a restaurant, you don't want the man at the next table to smoke until you've finished eating.

Asking people to do things

- ► Could you . . . please?
- ► . . . , will you?
- ► I wonder if you'd mind . . . , (-ing)?
- ► Can you . . . , please?
- ►*Would you mind . . . (-ing)?

► Grade these forms from 1 to 5 according to their level of formality. Give 1 for the most informal and 5 for the most formal.
► Which forms would you use to ask someone to do a small favour, and which would you use to ask someone to do a big favour?

Answers can be found on page 116.

Agreeing

- ► . . . Yes, certainly.
- ► Yes, of course.
- ►*No, not at all.

Refusing

- ► I'm sorry but I can't.
- ► I'm afraid . . .
- ► I'm terribly sorry but . . .

* 'Mind' has the meaning of 'object to' or 'be annoyed by' in these questions, so a negative answer in response indicates agreement to the request.

2 Thanks

Thank people in the following situations:

1 A sales representative from one of your suppliers took you to a restaurant for lunch. He's just paid the bill.
2 Someone has just opened the door for you.
3 Your secretary has given you **another** pair of socks for Christmas.
4 You have just had dinner at your boss's house. It's time to go home.
5 Your colleague helped you write a very difficult report.

Thanking	Replies
▸ Thanks.	▸ You're welcome.
▸ Thank you (so much) for . . .	▸ Not at all.
▸ Thank you very much indeed.	▸ Don't mention it.
▸ That's very *kind of you.	▸ It is/was a pleasure.

* How many other words can you think of to say instead of 'kind'?

3 Offers of help

Offer help in the following situations:

1 Someone is carrying two heavy cases.
2 Your friend has been driving for hours and he's tired.
3 Your colleague is talking on one of his phones. The other phone is ringing.
4 Someone's car won't start. It needs a push.
5 A customer is visiting your home town next month. He'll need a hotel room.

Offering help	
▸ Shall I . . . ?	▸ Which form is only suitable for situations where you're offering to work alongside someone?
▸ Can I . . .	
▸ Do you want a hand?	
▸ Would you like me to . . . ?	

Accepting help	Refusing help
▸ Yes please. Thanks a lot.	▸ Thanks very much but there's no need.
▸ Oh, that'd be great.	▸ No, it's all right thank you.
▸ Thank you. That's very good of you.	▸ That's very kind of you but I can manage.

4 Permission

Ask people for permission to do things in the following situations:

1 Ask a colleague if you can smoke.
2 Ask your boss for two days off. (It's the busiest time of the year.)
3 Ask a friend to lend you his car this lunch time.
4 Ask a client if you can use his phone.
5 You want to leave the lesson early. Ask your teacher.

Asking for permission

- ▸ *Do you mind if I . . . ?
- ▸ May I . . . ?
- ▸ Could I possibly . . . ?
- ▸ Can I . . . ?
- ▸ I wonder if I might . . . ?

Granting permission

- ▸ Yes, certainly.
- ▸ *No, not at all.
- ▸ By all means.
- ▸ Yeah, go ahead.
- ▸ Yes, of course.
- ▸ Please do.

Refusing permission

- ▸ I'm sorry but you can't because . . .
- ▸ I'm afraid . . .
- ▸ Well, actually . . .
- ▸ I'd rather you didn't because . . .
- ▸ *I'm sorry but I do.

* see note on page 66.

- ▸ Which forms would you use:
  - a when you don't know the person very well?
  - b when you know the person well?
  - c if you were going to cause them a lot of trouble?
  - d if you were going to cause them little or no trouble?

- ▸ Which phrase is the most formal and which phrase is the least formal?

  Answers can be found on page 116.

18 Making arrangements

1 Invitations

1 Invite your colleague to have lunch with you in a local pub or restaurant.
2 Invite your boss to dinner at your home.
3 See if your friend wants to go jogging with you this evening. (It's raining.)
4 Perhaps your customer would like to see round your factory.
5 Suggest one of these events to your partner:

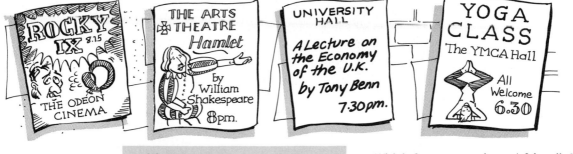

Inviting
▸ Do you feel like . . . (–ing)?
▸ How about . . . (–ing)?
▸ Do you fancy . . . (–ing)?
▸ Would you like to . . . ?
▸ I was wondering if you'd like to . . . ?

▸ Which forms sound most friendly?
▸ Which forms would you use with people you don't know very well?

Accepting
▸ Yes, I'd love to.
▸ *That'd be great. Thanks.

Refusing
▸ I'd love to but . . .
▸ That's very kind of you but unfortunately . . .
▸ Well, actually . . .

▸*'That'd be great.' What word is 'd short for?
▸ What other words can be used instead of 'great' in this sentence.

Answers on page 116.

> a Portuguese Maoist re-interpretation of Hamlet on roller-skates by the Rhondda Valley Friends of the Earth... Hmmm, sounds familiar.

2 Making an appointment

Caller

You want to make an appointment to see your solicitor, Mr Sanders, as soon as possible. Phone his office.

Receiver

You are Mr Sanders's secretary. Mr Sanders is a solicitor. He is on holiday at the moment but you expect him back next Tuesday. A client calls you.

> ▸ I'd like to make an appointment to see Mr Sanders.
> ▸ I'm afraid Mr Sanders is away at the moment.
> ▸ When will he be back? It's rather urgent.

3 The golf game

Caller

Phone your friend and see if he'd like to play golf with you some time next week. Fix a time.

Receiver

There's nothing you like more than playing golf. A friend calls you.

Ending a call

> **Checking the other person has nothing else to say**
> ▸ Right then . . . (pause) . . .
> ▸ O.K. . . . (pause) . . .
> ▸ Anyway . . . (pause) . . .

> **Finishing on a warm note**
> ▸ Thank you for calling.
> ▸ It was great to hear from you.
> ▸ Remember me to Mary and the children.
> ▸ Give my regards to Mrs Isaacs.

> **Referring to future contact**
> ▸ See you on Friday, then.
> ▸ Until Friday, then.
> ▸ I'll look forward to seeing you on Friday, then.

> ▸ Which of these phrases could you use to end a call from:
>   a a close friend?
>   b someone you don't know very well?

See page 116.

4 Fixing a time

Caller

You need to arrange a business meeting with your partner. Phone him/her to fix a time. Here's your diary for next week.

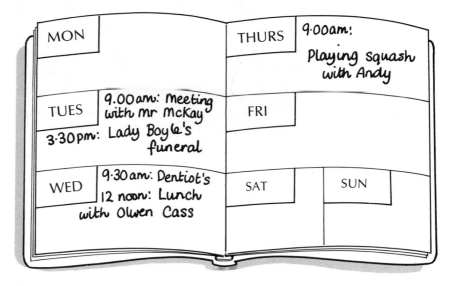

Receiver

You need to arrange a business meeting with your partner. He/She phones to fix a time. Turn to page 116 and look at your diary.

Suggesting a time

▸ When would | suit you?
▸ Would | Thursday | be convenient for you?
　　　　 | 3 o'clock |

▸ Are you free | on Wednesday?
　　　　　　 | at 1 o'clock?
　　　　　　 | in the afternoon?

▸ What about | 1 o'clock on Wednesday, then?
▸ Shall we say |

Saying yes

▸ Yes, I'm free at 1 o'clock.
▸ Yes, Wednesday would | be fine.
　　　　　　　　　　 | be convenient.
　　　　　　　　　　 | suit me.

Saying no

▸ I'm afraid | I can't make it | on Wednesday.
　　　　　 | I'm busy |
　　　　　 | I have another engagement |
　　　　　 | I've got something else on |

5 Changing plans

Caller

You have an appointment with your bank manager today but something else has come up and you can't make it.

Phone him, cancel today's appointment and arrange to see him tomorrow instead. it's very important that you see him tomorrow.

Receiver

You are a bank manager. An important client has an appointment to see you today. He phones to cancel it. Your schedule for tomorrow is on page 117.

Changing plans

▶ I'm afraid | I won't be able to make it.
something's come up.
I can't get out of. it.

▶ I'm sorry about this, but it's unavoidable.

▶ Could we make it tomorrow instead?

---

19 On the telephone

1 Telephone quiz   1

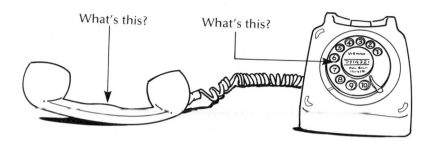

What's this?   What's this?

2 'Could you **telephone me** tomorrow?' How many other expressions can you think of to use, instead of 'telephone me'?

3 Supply the missing words:
  - He's always . . . the phone.
  - He . . . a lot of time . . . the phone.
  - He has to . . . a lot of phone calls.

4 Explain:
  - a switchboard
  - an extension
  - the code
  - a directory
  - a reverse charge call

5 What do these expressions mean?
  - I'll put you through.
  - His line's engaged.
  - Hold on.
  - She hung up.
  - We were cut off.

6 'Can I speak to Mr Tanner?'
  'I'm afraid he's . . . '
  How many reasons can you give for him not being able to take the call?

See page 117 for the answers.

He wants to know if we'll accept the charges.

2 Getting put through

Caller

Phone Saffron Building Supplies and ask to speak to:

Delphine Carey	Extension 294
Patrick Amos	Roofing department
Len Noon	Despatch department
Andrew Broadhead	Plumbing department
Vera Roberts	Extension 148
Margaret Abbot	Personnel department

> ▶ I'd like to speak to . . .
> ▶ Could you put me through to . . . ?
> ▶ Extension 294 please.
> ▶ I'll call back later.

Receiver

You are the switchboard operator at Saffron Building Supplies. Look at the information on page 117 and deal with the in-coming calls.

3 Leaving a message

Caller

Turn to page 118 for your instructions.

Receiver

You are Kenneth Butcher's secretary. Mr Butcher isn't in the office at the moment but you expect him back later this afternoon.

Identifying who's calling
> ▶ Is that . . . ?
> ▶ Who's calling?

Taking messages
> ▶ Would you like to leave a message?
> ▶ Shall I ask him to ring you when . . . ?

4 Taking down the details

Caller

You have received an urgent request from a customer for goods that you don't have in stock. Telephone your warehouse and ask for the items to be sent straight to the customer.

Customer: William Forsythe
 Company: Ascourt Electronics
 Address: Unit 4, Caxton Way
 Peterborough PE17 4XL
 Telephone: 0733 301771

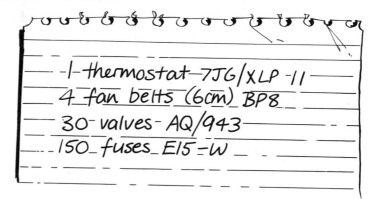

— -1- thermostat -7JG/XLP -11 —
4 fan belts (6cm) BP8
30 valves - AQ/943
150 fuses E15 -W

Starting	**Carrying on**
▸ Ready?	▸ O.K.?
	▸ Have you got that?

Finishing	**Checking**
▸ That's all.	▸ Do you want to read that back to me?
▸ That's the lot.	

Receiver

Turn to page 118 for your instructions.

Pronunciation: correcting

Correct the information, stressing the word that's wrong each time:
eg Did you say thirteen valves   AQ/943?
 No, I said THIRTY valves   AQ/943.

1 Did you say 13 valves   AQ/943?
2 Did you say 30 bulbs   AQ/943?
3 Did you say 30 valves   RQ/943?
4 Did you say 30 valves   AQ/953?
5 Did you say 30 valves   AQ/942?

5 Modern technology

Caller

You ordered a video camera from 'Hicks Teletape services' two weeks ago and it still hasn't arrived. Phone up and find out what has happened to it.

Receiver

Turn to page 118 for your instructions.

20 Information exchange

1 Getting information

Flight times

Caller

You want to know what time the flights from New York get into Heathrow today. Phone the British Airways Information desk and find out.

Receiver

You work for British Airways on their Information desk. Use the flight information on page 119 to answer an enquiry.

Hotels

Traveller

You are looking for somewhere to stay tonight. Go to the reception desk at the Tower Hotel, find out if they have any vacant rooms, how much they cost, and check in if you decide you like the hotel.

Receptionist

You work at the Tower Hotel. Use the information on page 119 to answer an enquiry from a traveller.

Exchange rates

Caller

You want to know how many American dollars you would get for £100, at today's exchange rates. Phone your bank and find out.

Receiver

You work in the foreign exchange department at a bank. Use the exchange rate information on page 119 to answer an enquiry.

Indirect questions	**Finding information**
▶ Could you tell me . . . ?	▶ Let's see . . .
▶ Could you possibly tell me . . . ?	▶ I'll just check that for you.
▶ Can you give me an idea of . . . ?	▶ Just a minute, I'll look it up.
	▶ I'll work it out.

2 Making enquiries

Caller

You bought this furniture from Matrix Ltd three years ago. You'd like to buy some more now. Phone them and see if they still make it. Check the prices as they have probably gone up.

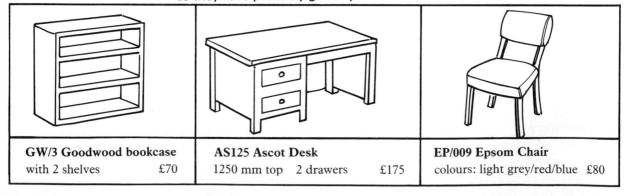

GW/3 Goodwood bookcase	**AS125 Ascot Desk**	**EP/009 Epsom Chair**
with 2 shelves £70	1250 mm top 2 drawers £175	colours: light grey/red/blue £80

> ▸ Do you still make/sell . . . ?
> ▸ Is it the same as . . . ?
> ▸ Have you changed . . . ?
> ▸ How much does it cost?

Receiver

Turn to page 120 for your instructions.

3 Placing an order

Caller

Phone Stationery Supplies Ltd and order the following items:

6 doz. black 'Scribo' felt tip pens @ 25p
3 doz. red 'Scribo' felt tip pens @ 27p
500 C6 envelopes (white) £20.16
90 blue 'Titan' files size A4 @ £1.65

Check the prices as you only have an old catalogue. Ask for your usual 7% discount and delivery this week.

> ▸ I'd like to place an order.
> ▸ I'd like . . .
> ▸ Could we have . . . ?
> ▸ Could I check the price of those?

Receiver

Turn to page 120 for your instructions.

4 At a trade fair

Salesman

You are running a stand at a trade fair. Someone who is interested in your products approaches you. Give him/her all the information you can and fill in your record form below.

Trade fair enquiries	
Caller's name:	Areas of interest:
Company:	
Dept:	
Address:	
	☐ Send brochures
Tel:	☐ Write
Telex:	☐ Send a quote

Welcoming callers

- ▸ Can I help you?
- ▸ I'm sorry, I didn't catch your name.
- ▸ Do sit down.
- ▸ Would you like a cup of coffee?

When you can't answer a question

- ▸ I'm afraid I can't tell you off hand.
- ▸ I think it's . . . , but I'll check that for you.
- ▸ I'll get Mr Scott to phone you/ send you a brochure.

Form filling

- ▸ Can I just take down your name?
- ▸ Could you tell me . . . ?
- ▸ Could you spell that?

Saying goodbye

- ▸ We'll be in touch.
- ▸ Don't hesitate to contact us if you think of anything else.

Caller

You are walking round a trade fair when you see your partner's stand. You approach him/her and ask for information about his/her product(s). Find out:

- as much as you can about the product(s)
- whether it/they would be worth buying for your company
- prices, delivery information, etc.
- about the after sales service

21 When things go wrong

1 Apologizing

Apologize in these situations:

1 You've just broken one of your host's wine glasses.
2 You've just trodden on the foot of the person standing next to you.
3 You lost your temper with your secretary yesterday.
4 You've opened one of your colleague's letters by mistake.
5 You didn't turn up for your appointment with a customer yesterday. Phone him/her and apologize.
6 You promised a customer their order would be delivered this Friday. You've just heard it won't be delivered until the following Tuesday. Phone them and explain.

Apologizing	**Accepting an apology**
► Sorry.	► It doesn't matter.
► I'm very sorry.	► It's O.K.
► I really am very sorry indeed.	► That's all right.
	► Don't worry about it.
	► Never mind.
	► These things happen.

2 Faulty goods

Caller
Turn to page 121 for your instructions.

Receiver
A customer phones you to complain about some telephone handsets he/she bought from you. Find out what the problems are and decide what you're going to do about them.

> ► What exactly seems to be the problem?
> ► Would you like | a replacement?
> | a refund?
> ► If you return it to us we can . . .

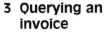

3 Querying an invoice

Caller
Turn to page 121 for your instructions.

Receiver
A customer phones to query an invoice you sent him/her. Here is a copy. Find out what's wrong.

```
 G. Ort                ST IVES COMPUTER STORE              020672
 3 Knights Close        Market Passage, St Ives, PE13 4NJ
 Great Brickhill          Tel. (0936) 43785 Tlx 693841    Your order no.
 Milton Keynes                                            Account no.
 Bucks MK7 94U                                            24 September

     QUANTITY    |          DESCRIPTION           |         PRICE
        1        | BBC Master Computer            |        450.00
        1        | Mitsubishi double disc drive   |        269.00
                 |            in plinth           |
        3        | Mitsubishi 1404 medium resolution |     970.00
                 |    colour monitors @ £290      |
        3        | 10 DS/DD 5¼" floppy discs      |         60.00
                 |            @ £20               |
 Payment within 30 days              TOTAL              1749.00
                                  VAT @ 15%              262.35
 VAT Reg No. 213 2382 09      Postage & packing           12.00
                                 Amount due             2023.35
```

Promising Action

► I'll | look into it | immediately.
     | sort it out | straight away.
     | have it | corrected |
     | | put right |

4 Making excuses You've got problems! See if you can talk your way out of these situations. You might need a few minutes to prepare a good excuse.

1 You're two hours late for an appointment because you overslept, but you can't tell your customer that. Lie convincingly.

2 TV news coverage of the arrival in London of the President also shows you and your secretary getting off the flight from Paris together. You told your wife you'd been to Brussels alone. Explain yourself.

3 Explain why you're fiddling in the office charity collecting box with a knife and pencil.

4 Two months ago you promised to give an after dinner speech at the Rotary Club, but you forgot to write the date in your diary. The Rotary Club President is on the phone now asking why you didn't turn up last night.

5 You told your boss you had to have a long weekend off in order to attend your aunt's funeral. You have returned to work two days late with a sun tan and a broken leg. Your boss knows you like skiing holidays and he/she's extremely suspicious.

6 While waiting for the Personnel Manager in his/her office, you see a file with your name on it on his/her desk. It's labelled 'Private and Confidential'. You've just opened it and started reading when he/she walks in.

► I meant to . . . , but unfortunately . . .
► I didn't intend to . . . but . . .
► I didn't realize that . . .
► Nobody told me that . . .

22 Out and about

1 Restaurants

You're taking a customer out to lunch at a restaurant.

Before you go:
1 Phone the restaurant and book a table.

When you arrive:
2 Identify yourself to the waiter.

When you're ordering the meal:
3 Find out what type of soup 'Soup of the Day' is.
4 You see 'Whitebait' on the menu, but you don't know what it is. Ask the waiter.
5 Ask for the wine list.

During the meal:
6 Ask for some water.
7 You ordered roast duckling but the waiter is serving you with something that looks like chicken casserole.
8 Ask your guest for the salt.
9 Offer your guest some more wine.
10 You are still waiting for the water!

At the end of the meal:
11 Ask for the bill.
12 Ask the waiter to get you a taxi.
13 Your guest thanks you for the meal. Reply.
14 The bill arrives but it's incorrect. You had three bottles of wine, not four.
15 You realize your credit card is out of date.

MENU

Starters

Soup of the day	£ 3.50
Whitebait with brown bread and butter	£ 6.50
Liver pâte with toast	£ 3.90

Main Courses

Chicken casserole	£ 8.90
Grilled lamb chops	£10.90
Roast beef and Yorkshire pudding	£12.50
Roast duckling with cherry sauce	£11.60

Choice of fresh vegetables
Roast, boiled or jacket potatoes

Sweets from the trolley
Cheese and biscuits   £ 3.50

★   Coffee   ★   Liqueurs   ★

Service
not included

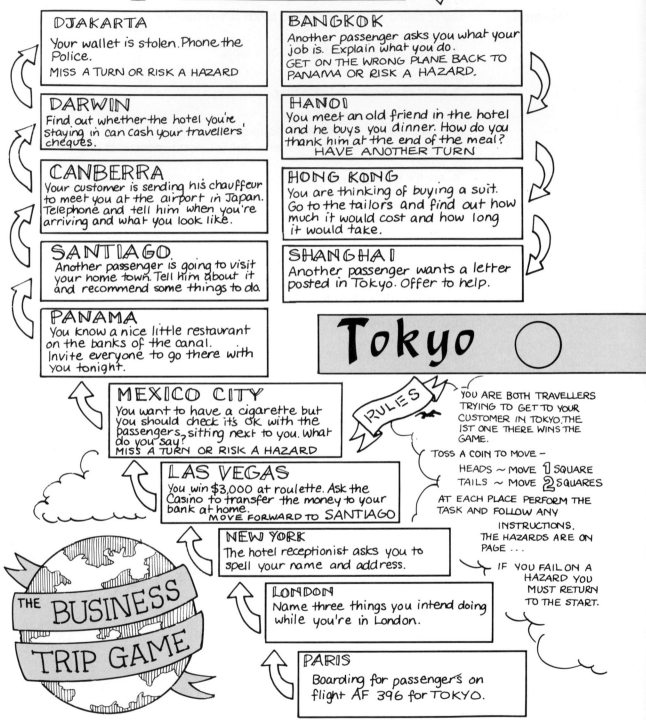

SINGAPORE
You decide to stay at the Hilton. Phone the hotel and make a reservation.

DJAKARTA
Your wallet is stolen. Phone the Police.
MISS A TURN OR RISK A HAZARD

BANGKOK
Another passenger asks you what your job is. Explain what you do.
GET ON THE WRONG PLANE BACK TO PANAMA OR RISK A HAZARD.

DARWIN
Find out whether the hotel you're staying in can cash your travellers' cheques.

HANOI
You meet an old friend in the hotel and he buys you dinner. How do you thank him at the end of the meal?
HAVE ANOTHER TURN

CANBERRA
Your customer is sending his chauffeur to meet you at the airport in Japan. Telephone and tell him when you're arriving and what you look like.

HONG KONG
You are thinking of buying a suit. Go to the tailors and find out how much it would cost and how long it would take.

SANTIAGO
Another passenger is going to visit your home town. Tell him about it and recommend some things to do.

SHANGHAI
Another passenger wants a letter posted in Tokyo. Offer to help.

PANAMA
You know a nice little restaurant on the banks of the canal. Invite everyone to go there with you tonight.

Tokyo ◯

MEXICO CITY
You want to have a cigarette but you should check it's ok with the passengers sitting next to you. What do you say?
MISS A TURN OR RISK A HAZARD

LAS VEGAS
You win $3,000 at roulette. Ask the Casino to transfer the money to your bank at home.
MOVE FORWARD TO SANTIAGO

NEW YORK
The hotel receptionist asks you to spell your name and address.

LONDON
Name three things you intend doing while you're in London.

PARIS
Boarding for passengers on flight AF 396 for TOKYO.

THE BUSINESS TRIP GAME

RULES
YOU ARE BOTH TRAVELLERS TRYING TO GET TO YOUR CUSTOMER IN TOKYO. THE 1ST ONE THERE WINS THE GAME.

TOSS A COIN TO MOVE —
HEADS ~ MOVE 1 SQUARE
TAILS ~ MOVE 2 SQUARES

AT EACH PLACE PERFORM THE TASK AND FOLLOW ANY INSTRUCTIONS.
THE HAZARDS ARE ON PAGE . . .

IF YOU FAIL ON A HAZARD YOU MUST RETURN TO THE START.

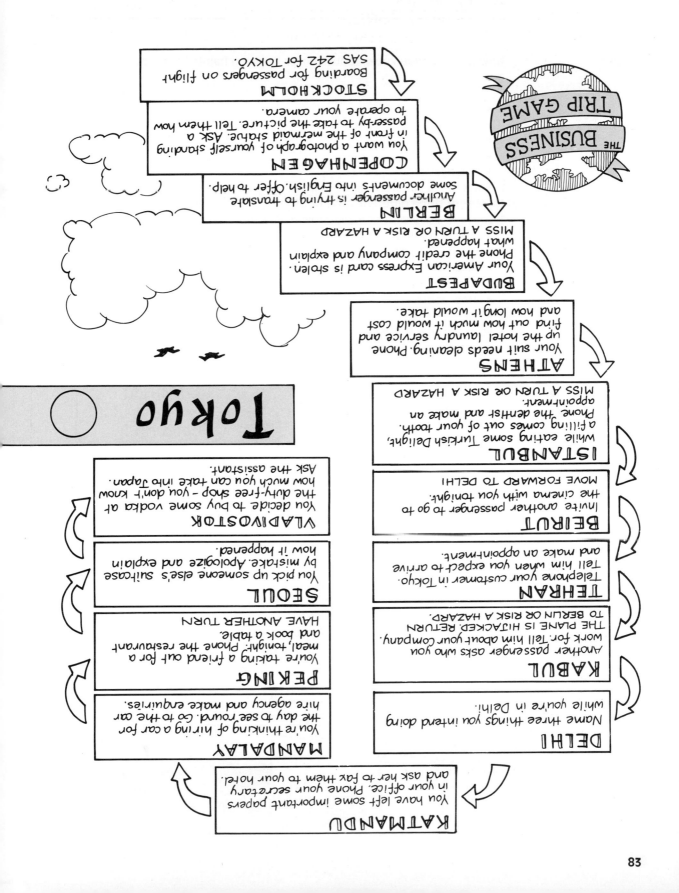

THE BUSINESS TRIP GAME

Tokyo

STOCKHOLM
Boarding for passengers on flight SAS 242 for TOKYO.

COPENHAGEN
You want a photograph of yourself standing in front of the mermaid statue. Ask a passer-by to take the picture. Tell them how to operate your camera.

BERLIN
Another passenger is trying to translate some documents into English. Offer to help.

BUDAPEST
Your American Express card is stolen. Phone the credit company and explain what happened.
MISS A TURN OR RISK A HAZARD

ATHENS
Your suit needs cleaning. Phone up the hotel laundry service and find out how much it would cost and how long it would take.

ISTANBUL
While eating some Turkish Delight, a filling comes out of your tooth. Phone the dentist and make an appointment.
MISS A TURN OR RISK A HAZARD

BEIRUT
Invite another passenger to go to the cinema with you tonight.
MOVE FORWARD TO DELHI.

TEHRAN
Telephone your customer in Tokyo. Tell him when you expect to arrive and make an appointment.

KABUL
Another passenger asks who you work for. Tell him about your company.
THE PLANE IS HIJACKED. RETURN TO BERLIN OR RISK A HAZARD.

DELHI
Name three things you intend doing while you're in Delhi.

KATMANDU
You have left some important papers in your office. Phone your secretary and ask her to fax them to your hotel.

MANDALAY
You're thinking of hiring a car for the day to see round. Go to the car hire agency and make enquiries.

PEKING
You're taking a friend out for a meal tonight. Phone the restaurant and book a table.
HAVE ANOTHER TURN

SEOUL
You pick up someone else's suitcase by mistake. Apologize and explain how it happened.

VLADIVOSTOK
You decide to buy some vodka at the duty-free shop – you don't know how much you can take into Japan. Ask the assistant.

83

3 Pubs

How much do you know about English drinking habits? Test yourself with this quiz.

1 What is:
- a pint?
- a local?
- a landlord?
- a round?
- a hangover?

2 Name three different types of beer.

3 Think of three different ways of offering drinks to your companions.

4 You're in a pub with an English friend. How would you reply when he/she says:
- 'I'll get the first one in'
- 'What's it to be?'
- 'Cheers!'
- 'Same again?'
- 'How about a game of darts?'
- 'One for the road?'

5 You overhear these snips of conversation in the pub. What do you think the speakers mean?

> I'd like a soft drink, please.

> I'm afraid it's got a bit of a head on it.

> Down that quickly and I'll get you another.

> It's your shout.

> I'm just going to spend a penny.

6 What's the difference between:
- draught and bottled?
- opening time and drinking-up time?
- a tied house and a free house?
- being tipsy and being plastered?
- a drop of the hard stuff and a wee dram?

Possible answers can be found on page 122.

> Same again, Brian?

PART THREE – GROUP WORK

23 Leading the group

1 Expressing opinions

Give an instant opinion on one of the topics below, then ask the other members of the group what they think:

eg It seems to me that private schools are a bad thing because they give the children of the rich a huge advantage! What's your reaction to that, Michael?

- private schools
- football hooligans
- nuclear power
- computers
- smoking in public places

- military service
- capital punishment
- banks
- unemployment
- marriage

Look at these phrases and decide how strongly the speaker is asserting his or her views. Put them in the appropriate box.

I think . . . I don't think . . . I'm quite certain that . . . I would have thought . . . I don't doubt that . . . I believe . . . I feel sure that . . . My impression is that . . . As I see it . . . It seems to me that . . . It strikes me that . . .	Weak
	Medium
	Strong

Answers on page 123.

Asking for an opinion

- ► Michael, what's your reaction to that?
- ► Terry, how do you feel about this?
- ► Any comments, Mary?
- ► Brian, do you have any strong feelings on this?
- ► What do you think about this, Sue?
- ► Barbara, what are your views on that?
- ► Do you have any ideas on this, Alan?
- ► Elizabeth?

▸ How would you change these phrases if you were directing them at a group rather than an individual?

eg What's the general reaction to that?

How does everyone react to that?

2 Leading a discussion

Prepare to give a short informal talk to the group and lead a discussion to follow it. Questions must be provocative. The group will interrupt your talk as often as possible to ask questions and express their views.

These are some ideas for topics. You can choose one of them or you may decide to talk about something else:

- housing
- energy conservation
- sport
- crime
- an event in the news

- driving rules and habits
- privatization
- communism
- health and fitness
- family problems faced by hard-working executives

Interrupting

▸ (Excuse me) Can I just | say . . . ?
| ask . . . ?
▸ Could I come in here?
▸ Sorry to interrupt but . . .
▸ Yes, but . . .
▸ Er . . .

Stopping interruptions

▸ If I could just finish . . .
▸ If you'd let me finish . . .
▸ Just a minute . . .
▸ *Hang on . . .
▸ Listen . . .

* informal

"Sorry to interrupt, but could you turn the anaesthetic up a bit?"

3 Giving reasons

Tell the group:
- why you like your job
- why you married your husband/wife
- why you bought your house
- why you buy a particular newspaper
- why you like your car
- why you are learning English
- why you voted the way you did in the last election

<table>
<tr><td colspan="2">Giving reasons</td></tr>
<tr><td>► Firstly . . .</td><td>Secondly . . .</td></tr>
<tr><td>► One reason is . . .</td><td>Another is . . .</td></tr>
<tr><td>► To start with . . .</td><td>And on top of that . . .</td></tr>
<tr><td>► For one thing . . .</td><td>And for another . . .</td></tr>
</table>

4 Persuading

Role A

Persuade the group to do what you want. You have just invented a new breakfast cereal made from grass. You want everyone to:

- leave their highly paid jobs to form your new management team (you might like to decide what job each person would have in your new company)
- invest their money in the company

Prepare your arguments, and good luck!

Role B

Persuade the group to do what you want. You want them all to come away with you for a weekend on this holiday.

A WEEKEND OF MEDITATION
Find inner peace and tranquillity of mind

BOXWORTH HALL

Naturist Health Farm
FRIDAY–MONDAY   **£525**

The price includes:

4 x 5 hour lessons in meditation
Accommodation
Vegetarian meals
Ice baths
Use of all the health farm's facilities

Prepare your arguments, and good luck!

Role C

Persuade the group to do what you want. You are trying to raise money for charity. You are organizing a free fall parachute jump from an aeroplane at 2,000 feet.

You want them all to take part. All they have to do is:

• pay £15 for the jump (this price doesn't include insurance)
• find sponsors
• jump out of the plane
• pull the rip-cord
• collect the money from their sponsors and give it to you

You will give the money to your favourite charity: 'The Retired Bank Managers' Holiday Fund'. Present the idea to them and persuade them to take part.

Prepare your arguments, and good luck!

Role D

Persuade the group to do what you want. You want one of them to buy your second-hand car. Here are the details:

Price	£1,000
Model	British Leyland Mini 1000cc
Age	1966
Mileage	90,000 miles
Fuel consumption	25 m.p.g.

Think of some other special features it has to persuade the group it's a good bargain. You might have to reduce the price and/or lie a little bit.

Prepare your arguments, and good luck!

24 Achieving consensus

1 Government priorities

1 The place is Britain/Europe/. . . /and the time is now. What should the priorities of the government be?
2 Look at the tasks below. Think of two other tasks you would like them to complete.
3 Number the tasks in order of importance, giving 1 for the most important and 12 for the least important. Then compare your answers with the rest of the group. Try to reach a consensus.

	Your ranking	Group ranking
1 To invest in new industry		
2 To hold down inflation		
3 To minimize unemployment		
4 To reduce taxation		
5 To improve the public health service		
6 To promote the country's image abroad		
7 To tighten immigration policy		
8 To build up the defence forces		
9 To increase social benefits		
10 To set up a new education programme		
11		
12		

` Government Priorities <

Decide how the following phrases are used and put them in the appropriate box:

I agree completely. I wouldn't like to say. Yes, but . . . I couldn't agree more. You could be right. *Come off it. Up to a point but . . .	**Agreeing**
I'm inclined to agree with you on that. I'm afraid I can't go along with you on that. I can't say. Absolutely. Exactly, but don't you think that . . . .?	**Agreeing tentatively**
I suppose that's true. I think I agree. Perhaps. *You're dead right there. You have a point there but . . . I'm sorry but I really can't agree. *You must be joking.	**Being non-committal**
	Expressing reservations
	Disagreeing

* In what situations would you use these colloquial expressions?

Answers on page 124.

2 Exceptions to the rule

Decide whether these statements are generally true or false. Then consider exceptions to and limitations on the rule. What qualifications would you make?

Business management

1 Business failure is due to bad management.   True/False
2 All posts of responsibility within a company should be subject to election by the entire workforce every year.   True/False
3 The shares of a company should only be owned by the workers and management of that company.   True/False
4 A percentage of the annual profits/losses should be shared among the entire workforce.   True/False
5 Any worker should be allowed to study his company's accounts at any time.   True/False

Economic management

6 Once inflation is down the economy will pick up.   True/False
7 The government should invest in businesses whose products are likely to find a market.   True/False
8 Competition leads to bankruptcy. Bankruptcy leads to unemployment.   True/False
9 High levels of unemployment will continue for several decades. There's nothing we can do about it.   True/False
10 The unions are a major obstacle to economic recovery.   True/False

---

Generalizing

▶ In most cases,
▶ On the whole,
▶ In general,
▶ Broadly speaking,

business failure is due to bad management.

Introducing a contrasting point

▶ Still,
▶ All the same,
▶ However,
▶ On the other hand,

many other things can cause business failure.

Linking two contrasting points

▶ Some businesses fail | although / even though / in spite of the fact that | they're well managed.

---

3 The perfect manager

1 What makes a good manager? What personal qualities does the perfect manager have?

2 Think of two other important qualities to add to the list below.

3 Number the qualities in order of importance, giving 1 for the most important and 12 for the least important. Then compare your answers with everyone else and construct a group ranking.

	Your ranking	Group ranking
1 Intelligent and quick-thinking.		
2 Experienced and knowledgeable in his/her field.		
3 Friendly and sociable. Gets on well with everyone.		
4 Has charisma. Is able to inspire staff to work enthusiastically.		
5 Even-tempered. Doesn't get angry or annoyed easily.		
6 Tactful. Can handle people successfully without upsetting them.		
7 Good administrative skills. Deals with paperwork quickly and efficiently.		
8 Energetic and hard-working.		
9 Dresses well and always looks smart.		
10 Good sense of humour.		
11		
12		

4 What makes a bad manager? What personal qualities often prevent people from being good managers?

25 Teamwork

1 Suggesting a course of action

You are your company's think tank, meeting together to find ways of solving your company's problems. Brainstorm ideas for the problems below. Decide together which is the best course of action to follow.

1 Your company has some money to spend on improving its employees' English. What are the best ways of spending the money?
2 Your company owns a small field next to the factory. You will probably need it in a year or so if you extend the factory. What can you do with it in the meantime?
3 Your company employs five office cleaners who aren't needed for the next six weeks, but will be needed after that. What can you do with them in the meantime?
4 Your company has thrown out its tea and coffee machines and gone back to good old-fashioned china tea cups. You now have 50,000 unwanted plastic cups. What can you do with them?

Explaining the problem
- The question we've got to tackle is . . .
- We need to work out . . .
- The problem we're facing is . . .

Accepting an idea
- Yes, that's a good idea.
- Well that's worth a try.
- That sounds like a good idea.
- Great!

Making suggestions
- Shall we . . . (do)?
- Why don't we . . . (do)?
- Could(n't) we . . . (do)?
- How about . . . (doing)?
- Suppose we . . . (do/did)?
- What if we . . . (do/did)?

Raising objections
- Yes, but . . .
- That might be all right but . . .
- It's a good idea but . . .
- I'm not sure about that because . . .

2 Advice

Take it in turns to ask for and give advice. One person explains a problem while the others suggest solutions.

1 You have run up debts of £2,500 on your credit cards.
2 You can't get to sleep at night.
3 You want to go back to work after fifteen years off raising your children. Your previous job was Assistant Marketing Manager in a chemical company.
4 You are in love with someone who works in the same office, who never seems to notice you.
5 Your car won't start in the mornings.
6 You have just discovered your husband/wife owes $8,000 in gambling debts.

Giving advice

▸ Have you ever thought of . . . (-ing)?
▸ Why don't you . . .
▸ You could always . . .
▸ Your best bet is to . . .
▸ If I were you I'd . . .
▸ You should . . .
▸ You'd better . . .

▸ Which form is colloquial?
▸ Which two forms are stronger and more forceful?
▸ Which three forms are weaker?
▸ In what situations would you use strong and weak forms?
▸ 'If I were you I'd . . . '
  'You'd better . . . '
  What is 'd short for in these examples?

Answers on page 124.

3 Solving problems together

The group has to solve these problems. Suggest solutions, decide what to do and then decide which member of the group should do it.
eg We'll have to work out how to use the machine without the manual.
    No, I think we should find a translator.
    Will you do that, then?

1 The instruction manual for your latest piece of equipment is in Japanese.
2 The company car won't start. You all have to be in Manchester for a meeting at 3.30 p.m.
3 You need to post a parcel tonight and you've run out of stamps.
4 The photocopier has broken down.
5 Your boss's retirement party starts in half an hour. You can't find the gold watch you bought him.

Making suggestions	Deciding who should do it
▶ We'll have to . . . ▶ I think we should . . . ▶ We'd better . . .	▶ Will you do that, then? ▶ Can we leave that to you? ▶ Would you like me to deal with it? ▶ Shall I sort it out?

4 Motivation

1 How important is staff motivation to your company's profitability and success?

2 What motivates people to work that extra bit harder? Consider these factors:
  • ownership of company shares
  • increases in pay linked to the achievement of targets
  • frequent training courses
  • praise
  • opportunities for promotion
  • the threat of redundancy
  • being given more responsibility

3 Which of these factors would motivate you to work even harder than you do now? Compare your answers with the group.

4 Working together, think of some practical ways in which staff motivation in your company could be improved.

26 Decision-making

Board meeting to be held in the conference room
at 2.00 p.m. on Monday, 7th August, 1989

AGENDA
1 Minutes of the last meeting.
2 Measures to be taken to cut running costs.
3 How the measures are to be implemented.
4 Any other business.

You have the difficult job of reducing your company's running costs by £10,000. You will be holding a meeting to decide what measures to take. Read through the alternatives below and decide which ones you are in favour of. (You might be able to think of some alternative cost-cutting measures to add to the list.)

Get your arguments ready so that you can propose the alternatives you think best at the meeting.

	Estimated saving
1 Reduce the research and development budget:	
• by 2%	£1,720
• by 5%	£4,300
• by 10%	£8,600
2 Reduce the staff training budget:	
• by 5%	£1,125
• by 10%	£2,250
• by 15%	£3,375
3 Reduce temperatures throughout the building to:	
• 20°C	£1,250
• 17½°C	£3,000
• 15°C	£5,800
4 Reduce travelling costs by:	
• travelling economy class instead of business class on flights	£2,420
• taking away all company cars and having a car pool instead	£4,500
5 Reduce telephone bills by not allowing any external calls to be made before 1 p.m.	£1,310
6 Stop sponsorship of local football team	£450
7 Stop giving company diaries and calendars to customers	£1,960
8 Cancel the staff Christmas dinner and dance	£3,980
9 Make the company cleaning staff redundant and contract the work out to independent operators	£2,800
10 Stop provision of free tea and coffee and install hot drink machines	£1,600

▶ Compare these phrases with the ones on page 95 for making suggestions.
▶ How are they similar and how are they different?
▶ In what situations would you use them?

Putting forward proposals
▶ I propose that we . . .
▶ I recommend that we . . .
▶ I suggest that we . . .

Decide how these phrases are used to reply to proposals and put them in the appropriate box.

Yes, I'm in favour of that. I'm sorry but I'm not very happy about that. I see what you want to do but . . . I can't go along with that. There doesn't seem to be much choice. That's got to be the best option/ solution. We have no alternative. I'm afraid that might not be feasible because . . . That's just not on. I suppose that's our only option. That's a very good idea. I've got a few reservations about that because . . .	**Accepting**
	Accepting reluctantly
	Raising objections
	Rejecting

Answers on page 124.

2 Legal responsibility

You are judges. You must decide whether the following companies have done anything wrong, legally or morally.

If they have broken a law, decide what the crime is and what the punishment should be. If they haven't broken a law, have they done anything morally wrong? How can the situation be resolved and prevented from happening again in the future?

1 A multinational chemical company failed to maintain adequate safety standards at a factory owned by its subsidiary in the Third World. A poisonous gas leak led to the death of 500 people and a further 5,000 people were severely disabled.
2 An electrical company bribed a government official in order to get a contract to wire a new public building.
3 Five large airline companies reached an agreement that they should reduce their prices in order to drive a smaller competitor out of business. Once their competitor was bankrupt they increased their prices again.
4 A pharmaceutical company marketed drugs which had not been tested sufficiently. As a result of using one of their products 5,000 pregnant women gave birth to deformed babies.
5 A credit information company wrongly blacklisted the owner of a small business. As a result of their error, his creditors foreclosed and he went bankrupt. His ten employees lost their jobs and the man shot himself.
6 A manufacturer of microwave ovens sold its goods without warnings that live animals should not be placed in the ovens. Someone claims to have lost a miniature dog worth $2,000, while trying to dry its hair.

Making points
► The | main / essential / crucial / interesting | point / thing | is . . .

Being non-committal
► It's difficult to say for sure.
► It's very hard to say.
► I can't comment on that.
► I wouldn't know about that.

3 Business ethics questionnaire

'A gentleman's word is his bond', but how honest are you in your business dealings? Test yourselves with this questionnaire, making sure you reach an agreement on each answer.

Turn to page 125 to check your answers.

1 You are research scientists. You have discovered a wonderful new product which could make you dollar millionaires in three years. However, the discovery was made during company time and using company equipment. It states clearly in your contract that all patent rights for new products belong to the company.

Will you:
a. tell the company all about your discovery and let them develop it?
b. tell the company you have discovered something big but refuse to give details until you have negotiated patent rights and/or a substantial increase in pay?
c. leave the company without telling them about your invention and start your own business manufacturing the product?

2   You are union members. Your union has instructed all members to strike for one day in support of a fellow worker who was wrongfully dismissed. Although the company didn't follow the letter of the law in this case, you have little sympathy with the man who was dismissed.

Will you:
a.   go on strike?
b.   arrange to take the day off as holiday?
c.   work as normal?

3   You have employed ten school leavers in your shop for the past year on the government's Youth Training Scheme. They restock the shelves and work the tills, for which they receive £28.50 a week (much less than other employees doing the same job).

They are all good workers but now the training scheme's year is up and you must decide what to do.

Will you:
a.   take them onto your normal payroll, paying them the same wages as the other workers?
b.   offer to let them continue working for you, but at a lower wage than the other workers?
c.   say goodbye to them and take on another ten school leavers on the Youth Training Scheme, who you only need to pay £28.50 a week?

4   When your boss is calculating your holiday entitlement you discover to your surprise that the three days you had off last August have not been recorded. Your boss has obviously forgotten about them.

Will you:
a.   remind him about the three days?
b.   ask him to re-check his figures then if he still doesn't remember, keep quiet about it?
c.   think yourself lucky and take the extra three days off?

5   One of the men in your department has told you that he is applying for another job and that he put your name down as referee on his application. (He apologized for not asking your permission but explained that you were on holiday at the time.)

As it happens you want him to get a different job as you feel he is incompetent and you have to waste a lot of time checking his work.

When you are asked to supply a reference will you:
a.   say what you really think about the man's work?
b.   write about his few good points and say nothing about his failings?
c.   give him a glowing reference so he'll get the other job and leave your staff?

6   You work for a company that rewards staff loyalty. You are applying for jobs with a competitor and need time off to attend interviews.

Will you:
a.   ask for the time off and tell the truth about where you are going?
b.   arrange to take the day off and if asked, lie about where you are going?
c.   wait till the day of the interview and then call in sick?

7 You are middle managers in a company which is at present engaged in a dispute with its workforce over a reduction in pay.

The union is calling its members out on strike next week for an unspecified length of time. Your boss has instructed you to employ 'blackleg' labour although you have pointed out that this will lead to bitterness and resentment for years to come.

Will you:
  a. employ blackleg labour?
  b. go through the motions of trying to employ blacklegs, but make sure you fail?
  c. refuse to follow your boss's instructions?

8 You are the owners of a small company. You have just bought some very expensive carpets for your homes and some much cheaper carpets for your offices. It would be very easy to swap the receipts and charge the company for the more expensive carpets. You don't think the tax man would catch you.

Will you:
  a. be honest and just charge the company for the office carpets?
  b. swap the receipts and pay for the cheaper office carpets yourselves?
  c. charge all the carpets to the company?

9 Your company is going to build a new factory in the Middle East and you are responsible for examining the tenders from all the contractors interested in building the new plant. The two best tenders are of equal merit, and you were intending to recommend them both and let the Board decide.

But this morning you received a phone call from Emporium, one of the two contractors on the shortlist. They indicated that a large sum of money had been deposited in a Swiss bank account, to be withdrawn by you if they get the contract.

Will you:
  a. recommend the two tenders as you intended but tell the board about Emporium's commission/bribe?
  b. recommend the two tenders as you intended, but keep quiet about the commission. Then, if Emporium get the contract, accept the commission?
  c. recommend that Emporium is given the contract and claim your commission?

10 Last year one of your suppliers sent you a case of champagne as a Christmas present, but it didn't arrive. Presumably it was lost in transit. Your supplier claimed for a new case from his insurance company which you received last week.

You have just been cleaning out a store room and to your surprise, you have found the first case of champagne. It was delivered after all, but you had forgotten about it.

Will you:
  a. phone your supplier and explain your mistake?
  b. keep quiet about it and enjoy another case of champagne?
  c. phone your supplier and tell him the second case hasn't arrived either?

27 Creative planning

1 Build your own utopia

You are a civilian cabinet which has taken over from the military junta which governed your country from 1984 to the present time. During this period all democratic rights were suspended. The cabinet now has absolute power to decide the country's future. Consider the following and reach an agreement.

1 Elections:
- how often?
- who should and shouldn't have the vote?
- should voting be compulsory?

2 The monarchy:
- should the monarchy be restored?
- should there be a president? (and if so what kind?)

3 Nationalization: what services and industries should the state run:
- education?
- health?
- the railways?
- electricity?
- telecommunications?
- distilleries and breweries?

4 Taxation:
- how should citizens be taxed?

2 Scotch whisky campaign

You all work for an advertising agency. You are responsible for the launch of a new product onto the market: a fine blend of Scotch whisky. The distillery is prepared to spend as much money as is necessary to ensure a good launch for their product.

1 Together you must decide:

a what sort of people will buy the product –
- age?
- sex?
- income group?

b what sort of image you want the product to have –
- high quality?
- good taste?
- typically Scottish?
- made in the old traditional way?
- high tech formula?
- makes you attractive to the opposite sex?
- drunk by rich/famous/glamorous people?
- good value for money?
- anything else?

c where it will be advertised –
- television?
- magazines and newspapers (which ones)?
- bill boards?
- direct mail shots?
- anywhere else?

(continued overleaf)

2 Think of a brand name for the whisky.
3 Design the bottle and packaging.
4 Make up a sales slogan.
5 Design a magazine/newspaper advertisement or script a television/radio advertisement and then perform it.

Riddle

It's spelt with an 'e' in Ireland.
It's spelt without an 'e' in Scotland.
How is it spelt in the USA?

Answer on page 126.

Self study: word building

BARGAIN
Six words for the price of one

Several different English words can sometimes be formed from the same root. This can be a great help when you want to expand your vocabulary. But you need to be careful about pronunciation. The stress can change position in the different words.

Using a good dictionary, complete the table below and mark where the main stress falls in each word

Answers on page 126.

The name of the activity	the person	the object(s) involved	the action	the adjective
advertising	advertiser	an ad an advert an advertisement	to advertise	—
	producer			
selling		a sale sales		saleable
			to purchase	—
consumption		—		consumable
	distributor	—		
industrialization			to industrialize	industrial industrious
negotiating negotiation		—		

3 The ideal workplace

The building

What makes a building a good place to work in?

How important are the factors below?

Give each one a score from 0 (not important) to 10 (very important). Compare your answers with the group.

	Your score (0–10)	Group score (0–10)
1 Plenty of space		
2 Clean and tidy		
3 Good heating and lighting		
4 Nicely decorated		
5 Attractive and comfortable furniture		
6 Separate staff smoking room		
7 Good canteen		
8 Good car parking facilities		

Your office

Draw a plan of your office indicating where the furniture is.

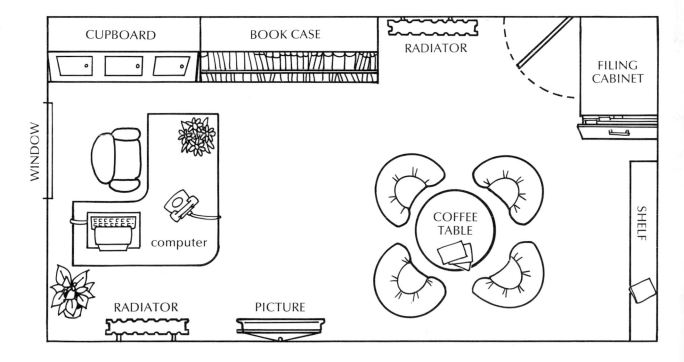

Work with a partner. Describe your plan to them so that they can draw it. (Don't show them the plan, just tell them about it!) When they have finished, compare the two plans and discuss any differences. Explain what you like and don't like about your office.

The ideal office

Together as a group, draw a plan of the perfect office. Spare no expense to create the office you would all like to work in. Consider:

- how much space you need
- lighting
- heating
- the equipment you would like
- the furniture:
  what pieces of furniture you want, what styles of furniture you want, where you want it positioned.
- the decoration:
  walls, ceiling, floor, upholstery, curtains, etc.
- extra decorative features, e.g. mirrors, pictures, plants, etc.

4 A men's magazine

Deep End Publishing are launching a new magazine for men between the ages of 25 and 35, to appeal to a broad range of interests. You are the editorial group, meeting to decide the format of the magazine.

1 Who will read the magazine?
  Take a 'typical' reader. Work out his:
  - income bracket
  - education
  - car
  - hobbies
  - family situation
  - where he lives

2 What will the magazine look like?
  - glossy?
  - how many pages?
  - size?
  - colour?
  - how much advertising? etc.

3 What features will it include?
  - interviews (who with?)
  - fiction (what type?)
  - fashion (what type?)
  - DIY (examples?)
  - pin ups
  - the arts (which?)
  - sports (what?)

  - political comment (for example?)
  - male beauty pages
  - problems page
  - cookery (what sort of dishes?)
  - business information (what sort?)
  - horoscopes
  - anything else

4 What will you call your magazine?

5 How will you launch and market it?
  - free copies
  - test market one area
  - TV advertising
  - price
  - weekly/monthly issue

28 Negotiations

1 True or false

Decide whether these statements are true or false and compare your answers with the group.

1 You need really good English to succeed in a negotiation. True/False

2 It's easier to negotiate with other non-native speakers of English than with native speakers. True/False

3 Some nationalities are easier to negotiate with than others. True/False

4 It's easier to negotiate in teams than on your own. True/False

5 The buyer usually has the advantage over the seller in a negotiation. True/False

6 Failure in a negotiation is often caused by not being well enough prepared. True/False

2 Discounts

Customer

You use 3,000 cellophane boxes a month and you need to order some more from your supplier. You can buy enough boxes for several months at once if he/she gives you a large enough discount. Find out what he/she's offering and negotiate a deal.

Supplier

Your company makes cellophane boxes. One of your customers phones you to enquire about discounts for bulk purchases. Use the chart on page 126 to explain how much discount he/she can get.

Making conditions		
▸ We give a 10% discount	if but only if on condition that as long as providing	the customer orders 5,000.
▸ We never give a 10% discount	unless even if	

1 In one of these sentences, a customer who orders 5,000 doesn't get a discount. Which sentence is it?

2 Do you offer discounts for your customers? How are they calculated?

3 A contract of sale

You are interested in trading with one another. Set the scene. Decide:
● what goods are being sold
● who is the customer and who is the supplier
Negotiate a contract. Consider the following details. (Not all of them will be important.)

1 The goods:
  ● exactly what is being bought?
2 Packaging:
  ● how will the goods be packaged? (bear in mind climatic conditions, method of transport, legal, customs or shipping requirements, etc.)

107

3 Transport:
  - consider the possible alternatives
  - how much do they cost?
  - who will pay for what?

4 Delivery time:
  - when will the goods be shipped/delivered?
  - will all the goods be delivered at once or will delivery be made in instalments?

5 Insurance:
  - who will arrange and pay for insurance for the different stages of the journey?

6 Payment:
  - how and when will payment be made?
  - are there penalties for late delivery?

7 Price:
  - how much do the goods cost?
  - are discounts available?

Explaining your terms

▸ As a rule we . . .
▸ We don't usually . . .
▸ I'm afraid we never . . .

Asking questions

▸ Could you quote me CIF Rotterdam?
▸ What would that be FOB?
▸ Could you guarantee . . . ?
▸ Would you be able to . . . ?

4 A bank loan

Role A

You are a businessman meeting your bank manager for a loan.
Be prepared to tell him about your business. Also decide:
- why you need the money
    - *eg* to finance new plant or equipment
        to expand your present building
        to finance new stock
        to bridge the period between deliveries and payment
- how much money you want
- how and when you could afford to repay the money
- what security you can offer

Find out how much he is prepared to lend you and what the interest would be.

Role B

You are a bank manager. A client is applying for a loan. Find out:
- why he wants the loan
- how much money he wants
- how and when he intends to repay the loan (work out how much interest he would have to pay)
- whether his business is financially strong enough to ride a set-back
    - *eg* Could he survive a fall in sales or late payments from creditors?
- what security he can offer

Decide whether to give him the loan.

5 Union negotiations

Do you belong to a trade union? Would you ever join one? What is the secret of good management–union relations?

Setting the scene.

You are going to represent either the union or the management at an annual pay negotiation meeting. Before you begin, set the scene.

1 Decide where the negotiation is going to take place. It should be your own company, or a company you know well.

2 Go over the points below and establish the background to the negotiations. Add any other relevant details. Guess any figures you don't know.

The past	The present
any long standing disputes	% of workforce who are union members
last year's pay rise	
rate of inflation over the last year	present rates of pay (basic and overtime)
company profits for the last year	
any changes in work methods/ practices/conditions this year	pensions
	maternity pay and other benefits

The negotiation

Prepare your arguments in groups.

Union officials:

Decide what your goals are. For example:

- a pay increase: what %?
- longer holidays: how much longer?
- increased benefits: what?

Decide what your priorities are and set a minimum target below which you will not drop. (You can ask for more initially.) Be prepared to justify your demands.

Management representatives

Decide what you can afford to offer. Set limits for the maximum you are prepared to pay. (You can offer less initially.) You might want to propose a productivity deal or other measures to increase profits. Be prepared to justify your offer.

Getting the ball rolling

- ▶ Perhaps you'd like to start by telling us . . .
- ▶ What did you have in mind?
- ▶ What's your position on this?

Accepting offers

- ▶ That seems reasonable.
- ▶ We could agree to that.
- ▶ That should be all right.

Rejecting offers

- ▶ That seems to be rather high/low.
- ▶ That's not exactly what we had in mind.
- ▶ I'm afraid that's unacceptable.
- ▶ That's out of the question.

Ideas for continuing with your English studies

1 Take out a subscription to 'London Calling' available from the BBC at PO Box 76, Bush House, Strand, London, England, WC2B 4PH. Then tune in to the World Service on your radio, listening to some programmes and recording others for study later. If you have a cassette player in your car, you can fit in some listening practice as you drive along.

2 Keep a look out for any English films on the TV, and make sure you watch them. If you're watching a programme with subtitles at home, cover them up with sticky tape across the bottom of the screen.

3 Look out for English films at cinemas. Why not take your family along with you?

4 Get your teacher to recommend books for further study, then set aside a regular time each week to get on with it.

5 Take out a subscription to an English book club. It's usually better to select short light-hearted books for reading in a second language. You're more likely to finish them! Buy English magazines, journals and newspapers whenever you can.
If you want some really easy relaxing reading, Oxford University Press and other publishers produce 'graded readers', books written in simplified English specially for foreign students.

6 Join your nearest British Council Library.

7 Try to arrange a language swap. An English person living in your country may be happy to talk English with you in exchange for some conversation in your mother tongue.

8 Persuade your company to run some 'in-house' English classes. Or enrol at a local conversation class. In some countries you can even have English lessons over the telephone. Having regular lessons can help you stick at your studies.

9 Have an 'English Day' in your company, or an 'English Evening' at home with your family where everyone speaks English to each other. Involve your colleagues and family as much as possible in your language learning.

Answer key and role-play notes

Part one: One-to-one

1 The alphabet and telephone numbers
Alphabet pronunciation

/eɪ/	/iː/	/e/	/aɪ/	/əʊ/	/uː/	/ɑː/
A	B	F	I	O	Q	R
H	C	L	Y		U	
J	D	M			W	
K	E	N				
	G	S				
	P	X				
	T					
	V					

Z is pronounced zi in American English and zed in British English.

In British English O is pronounced 'oh' in telephone numbers. In American English it's pronounced 'zero'.

4 Mathematics
Twelve plus six, divided by nine, times ten, minus two, equals eighteen.

Three quarters, plus a half, minus two thirds, equals seven twelfths.

The square root of sixty-four, multiplied by three cubed, equals seventy-two.

Four point one two, divided by two, equals two point oh six.

Seventy-five, plus fifteen per cent, equals eighty-six point two five.

1 Complaints
Self study

MAKE		DO
a profit	a decision	damage
enquiries	a journey	business
a discovery	a suggestion	a favour
money	love	one's best
a loss	a choice	work
friends	a mistake	
a joke	excuses	
an offer	a telephone call	

2 The mousetrap

The mouse is kicked into the cage.

The cage is lifted up.

The mouse is punched onto the conveyor belt, carried along and dropped into the sugar.

It's picked up, placed in the cat's mouth and eaten.

**Unit 5
Machines**

1 Shapes

Shape	Adjective	Shape	Adjective
circle	circular/round	pyramid	pyramidal
square	square	cone	conical
rectangle	rectangular	sphere	spherical
oval/ellipse	oval/elliptical	tube	tubular
triangle	triangular	cylinder	cylindrical
semicircle	semicircular	Y-shape	Y-shaped
cube	cubic	mushroom-shape	mushroom-shaped

2 Dimension

1 A: radius   B: diameter   C: circumference

2 The box is 12 centimetres long.
The length of the box is 12 centimetres.

The box is 5 centimetres wide.
The width of the box is 5 centimetres.

The box is 8 centimetres deep.
The depth of the box is 8 centimetres.

The box weighs 3 kilograms.
The weight of the box is 3 kilograms.

3 2 by 4 by 3 metres
24 cubic metres
24 cubic metres
12 square metres

**Unit 7
Descriptions**

1 Places
Self study

COUNTABLE	UNCOUNTABLE
job	work
machine	machinery
pound (£)	money
fact	information
suggestion	advice
experiment	research
chair	furniture
car	traffic
	equipment

**Unit 11
Describing trends**

1 The economy

Upward movement	Downward movement
to go up	to go down
to rise	to fall
to increase	to decrease
to climb	to drop
to pick up	to decline
to reach a peak	to hit a low
a rise	*a fall*
an increase	*a decrease*
	a drop
	a decline

113

Getting better
to improve
to recover
an improvement
a recovery

Getting worse
to deteriorate
a deterioration

Horizontal movement
to remain stable
to even out
to bottom out

2 Company trends
Speed or rate of change

rapid	rapidly	fast
slow	slowly	slow
sudden	suddenly	fast
sharp	sharply	fast
steady	steadily	medium
gradual	gradually	slow
fast	fast	fast
steady	steadily	medium

Size of change

noticeable	noticeably	medium
substantial	substantially	large
considerable	considerably	large
slight	slightly	small
significant	significantly	medium
dramatic	dramatically	large
negligible	negligibly	small

**Unit 13
Future
possibilities**

2 Planning your manpower

If suggests you're not sure something will happen.
When suggests you're pretty certain something will happen.
In case is used with precautions that need to be taken to prevent future
    problems.
Until is used for situations that will continue up to a certain time in the future.
Till is more colloquial than **until**.
Unless is similar to **if not**. It suggests something will happen if it isn't stopped by
    something else.

3 Company forecast

I expect . . .	b
I feel confident that . . .	a
I doubt if . . .	c
I reckon . . .	b
I don't doubt that . . .	a
I'd be surprised if . . .	c
I wouldn't mind betting . . .	b

Definite	. . . is bound to . . .
	There'll be . . .
Likely	. . . will probably . . .
	It's likely that . . .
Possible	. . . might . . .
	. . . could . . .
Unlikely	. . . isn't likely to . . .
	. . . probably won't . . .
Definitely not	There won't be . . .
	There's no chance of . . .

Unit 15
Presentations

4 Questions

Answering questions — possible matchings:

I obviously didn't explain that clearly enough — You didn't listen properly.

Mmm. That's a very interesting question — Hold on a minute, I'm thinking of an answer.

I'm glad you raised that point — I want to say something else on that subject.

I'm afraid I don't know the answer to that one — Why did you have to ask that?

Let me put it another way — I'll say it again, so listen this time.

Part two: Pairwork

Unit 16
Social chit-chat

2 Striking up a conversation

Possible answers:

1 Yes, it's improved since yesterday, hasn't it?

2 I notice you're going to the Palace, Blackpool. Would you be going to the conference too?

3 Excuse me. Haven't we met before somewhere? Wasn't it at the trade fair last year?

4 Hello. I must say I enjoyed your talk very much. The bit I found particularly interesting was . . .

5 Hello. It was a very interesting morning, wasn't it?

4 Quick replies

Possible answers:

1 I'm fine thanks, and you?

2 It was a pleasure. I'm so glad you liked them.

3 I'm afraid I haven't.

4 No, not at all. Go ahead.

5 Very good indeed. Things are very busy just now.

6 No, why? Have you lost one?

7 Yeah, I'd love one. Where shall we go?

8 Yes, it's five past three.

9 How do you do?

10 That's kind of him. How is George?
11 Certainly. When do you want to go?
12 Rather well, thank you.
13 Black with two sugars please.
14 Cheerio then. See you later.

Unit 17
Politely does it

1 Requests

1 . . . will you?   2 Can you . . . ?   3 Could you . . . ?
4 Would you mind . . . ?   5 I wonder if . . . ?
The more formal forms are often used to ask for big favours.

4 Permission

'May I . . . ?', 'Can I . . . ?' and 'Do you mind . . . ?' are less formal and so used with people you know well, or in situations where little or no trouble will be caused.
'Yeah, go ahead' is very informal and 'By all means' is quite formal.

Unit 18
Making arrangements

1 Invitations

'Would you like to . . . ?' and 'I was wondering . . . ?' are most formal and used with people you don't know well.
'd is short for the word 'would'.
That'd be great/lovely/nice/terrific/smashing, etc.

3 The golf game

Most phrases can be used in either situation, but 'Give my regards to Mrs Isaacs' sounds more formal than 'Remember me to Mary and the children' and so would probably be used with acquaintances rather than close friends.

4 Fixing a time

Receiver Here is your diary for next week.

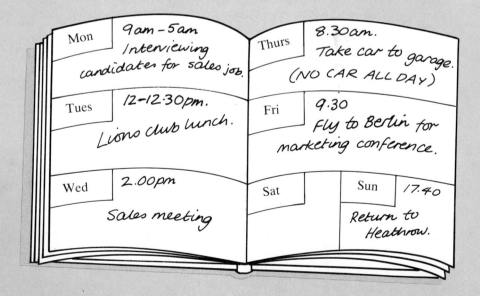

Mon	9am – 5am Interviewing candidates for sales job.
Tues	12–12.30pm. Lions club lunch.
Wed	2.00pm Sales meeting
Thurs	8.30am. Take car to garage. (NO CAR ALL DAY)
Fri	9.30 Fly to Berlin for marketing conference.
Sat	
Sun	17.40 Return to Heathrow.

5 Changing plans

Bank manager Here is your schedule for tomorrow.

9.30 – 12.30pm	Interviewing candidates for the position of assistant manager.
12.30 – 1.30pm	Lunch with your husband/wife. (It's your wedding anniversary.)
1.35pm	Catch the train to London.
3.00pm	AGM of the Bank's Board of Governors.
5.30pm	Cocktails with the Governor of the Bank of England.

**Unit 19
On the telephone**

1 Telephone quiz

1 a receiver, a dial

2 ring me/call me/phone me/give me a ring/give me a call

3 on/spends on/make

4 • Central board in a company where telephone connections are made.
 • Telephone connected to a switchboard but in another room.
 • Number coming before a telephone number *eg* international code, area code.
 • Book of telephone numbers.
 • Call for which the receiver pays (collect call in American English)

5 • I'll connect you.
 • The line is busy. He's already talking to someone.
 • Wait.
 • She finished the call.
 • The connection was broken.

6 Some possible answers: away today, out, at lunch, on holiday, not available, ill today, in a meeting.

2 Getting put through

Extension 294		engaged
Patrick Amos		on holiday
Dispatch department		at lunch
Andrew Broadhead		off sick
Extension 148		no answer
Margaret Abbot		in

▸ Do you know the extension number?
▸ I'm putting you through now
▸ The line's engaged
▸ It's ringing for you now
▸ Would you like to hold on?
▸ Could you phone again later?

3 Leaving a message

Caller

You have arranged to meet your colleague Ken Butcher for a drink tonight. However, you have just heard that you must leave for Scotland immediately on urgent business. Phone Ken at work and tell him you won't be able to make it.

Identifying yourself

▸ This is . . .
▸ . . . speaking

Leaving messages

▸ Can | you give him a message?
     | I leave a message?
     | you ask him to ring me
     | when . . . ?

---

4 Taking down the details

Receiver

You receive a telephone call from one of your sales offices. Take down the details of some items required by one of their customers. You'll need a pencil and some paper.

Starting

▸ Fire away.
▸ Go ahead.

Pausing

▸ Hang on.
▸ Just a minute.

Carrying on

▸ Yes.
▸ Got that.

Finishing

▸ Anything else?
▸ Is that the lot?

Checking

▸ Can I just check I've got that right?
▸ So that's . . .

---

5 Modern technology

Receiver

You are not a person. You are an answerphone machine at 'Hicks Teletape Services'. Explain to the caller that there is no one in the office at the moment and ask them to leave their message after the bleep.

**Unit 20
Information
exchange**

1 Getting information

LONDON HEATHROW

FLIGHT ARRIVALS

FLIGHT No:	TIME:	FROM:	DUE:
AE1314	09:45	FRANKFURT	09:45
BA2605	09:55	NEW YORK	10:15
TW9801	10:10	NEW YORK	DELAYED
LH4004	10:20	BERLIN	10:20
PA8220	10:25	NEW YORK	—

Bureau de Change
rates of exchange per £

		notes		cheques
		we sell	we buy	we buy
	AUSTRIA	21·60	22·95	22·15
	BELGIUM	64·60	68·35	66·20
	CANADA	1·85	1·96	1·9125
	FRANCE	10·40	11·00	10·65
	W. GERMANY	3·0675	3·2475	3·15
	GREECE	261·00	276·00	268·0
	HOLLAND	3·465	3·665	3·54
	ITALY	2235·00	2365·00	2275·00
	NORWAY	11·14	11·76	11·35
	PORTUGAL	257·00	271·00	263·0
	SPAIN	195·50	206·50	201
	SWEDEN	10·49	11·09	10·6
	SWITZERLAND	2·69	2·85	
	U.S.A.	1·5625	1·6575	1·59

**RATES SUBJECT
TO RESTRICTIONS**

TRANSACTION CHARGE

£1.50	£1.25	£1.50

The Tower Hotel

price per night

Single room	£45
Double room	£65
Single room with bath	£50
Double room with bath	£80

Prices include continental breakfast and VAT @ 17.5%

2 Making enquiries

Receiver

You work for Matrix Ltd, an office furniture company. A customer phones to enquire about your range of furniture. Here is part of your catalogue.

UPDATED NEW LINE

ALL SHELVES NOW ADJUSTABLE

GW/S Goodwood bookcase

with 2 adjustable
shelves   £80

NB125 Newbury desk EP/010

1250 mm top
3 drawers   £190

NOW AVAILABLE WITH OR WITHOUT ARMS

Epsom-X chair

Colours: light grey/red
blue/green/biege

with arms   £115
without arms   £85

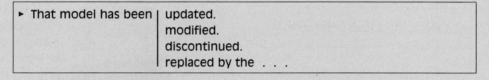

> ► That model has been │ updated.
> │ modified.
> │ discontinued.
> │ replaced by the . . .

Suggesting alternatives

► We've introduced a new model that might suit you better.
► You might be interested in the . . . instead.
► It's now available │ with arms │ as well.
│ in green │

3 Placing an order

Receiver

Check the items in your catalogue as you take the order.

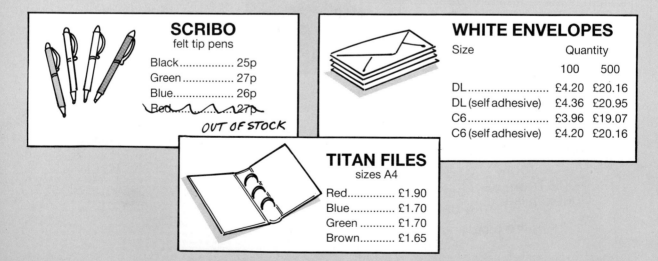

SCRIBO
felt tip pens

Black................. 25p
Green............... 27p
Blue.................. 26p
Red.................. 27p

OUT OF STOCK

WHITE ENVELOPES

Size	Quantity	
	100	500
DL........................	£4.20	£20.16
DL (self adhesive)	£4.36	£20.95
C6........................	£3.96	£19.07
C6 (self adhesive)	£4.20	£20.16

TITAN FILES
sizes A4

Red.............. £1.90
Blue............. £1.70
Green £1.70
Brown.......... £1.65

> ▶ I'm afraid | they're out of stock.
> | we've just had a big run on those.
> ▶ They should be in next week.

Unit 21
When things go wrong

2 Faulty goods

Caller

You took delivery of ten telephone handsets today. You have been trying them out and have found that three of them are faulty. Phone your supplier and complain.

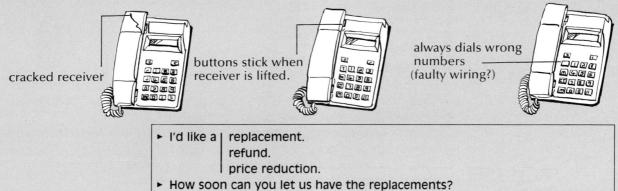

cracked receiver

buttons stick when receiver is lifted.

always dials wrong numbers (faulty wiring?)

> ▶ I'd like a | replacement.
> | refund.
> | price reduction.
> ▶ How soon can you let us have the replacements?

3 Querying an invoice

Caller

You have just received this invoice for some computer hardware that you ordered. There seem to be a few mistakes, and they have forgotten your 10% discount. Phone St Ives Computer Store and sort it out.

020672

G. Ort
3 Knights Close
Great Brickhill
Milton Keynes
Bucks MK7 94U

ST IVES COMPUTER STORE
Market Passage, St Ives, PE13 4NJ
Tel. (0936) 43785 Tlx 693841

Your order no.
Account no.
24 September

QUANTITY	DESCRIPTION	PRICE
1	BBC Master Computer	450.00 ✓
1	Mitsubishi double disc drive in plinth	269.00 ✓
3	Mitsubishi 1404 medium resolution colour monitors @ £290	970.00
3	10 DS/DD 5¼" floppy discs @ £20	60.00
	TOTAL	1749.00
Payment within 30 days	VAT @ 15%	262.35
	Postage & packing	12.00
VAT Reg No. 213 2382 09	Amount due	2023.35

(handwritten notes: £290 × 3 = £870; only two boxes delivered; 10% discount?)

Saying what's wrong

▶ There seems to have been a mistake.
▶ There's been a miscalculation.
▶ We ordered . . . but we only received . . .
▶ You haven't included our discount.

Putting it right

▶ I make that . . .
▶ That works out at . . .
▶ That should be . . .
▶ Shouldn't that be . . . ?

**Unit 22
Out and about**

2 The business trip game

Hazards

1 Your boss has heard about the £850 you spent in a night club and charged as a business expense. He/she wants you to explain it.
2 Your English teacher needs a holiday. Telephone and ask him/her to join you in the town you're in now.
3 You need to buy a present to give your Japanese customer. Think of something suitable you can buy in the town you're in now.
4 A customs officer has found a polythene bag in your luggage which contains a fine white powder. He thinks it's heroin. Explain what it is and what it's doing in your luggage.
5 Your husband/wife wants to join you on this business trip. Persuade him/her not to.
6 When you get off the plane you can't find your luggage. Complain to the airline official and find out what's happened to it.
7 You take a beautiful air hostess/handsome pilot out to a restaurant one night and bump into your mother-in-law. Think of an excuse fast!
8 You have paid extra to travel 'Business class', but when you get on the plane you find you're in a tourist seat. Complain to the air hostess.

3 Pubs

1 A measure of beer (about ½ a litre).
A nearby pub you visit regularly.
The owner or manager of a pub.
A drink for every member of a group.
The bad feeling you get after too much to drink the night before.
2 Lager, bitter, mild, stout, brown ale, light ale, pale ale.
3 What are you having?
What would you like to drink?
What can I get you?
4 (Possible answers)
No, no, let me.
A pint of bitter, please.
Cheers!

Yes please, but just a half this time.

Yes, I'd love one.

No thanks. I'd better not.

5 A soft drink is a non-alcoholic drink.

A head is the froth on top of a beer.

To down a drink is to finish it.

A shout is another word for a round.

To spend a penny is a euphemism for going to the toilet.

6 Draught beer comes from a barrel, not a bottle.

Drinking-up time is the time between when a pub stops serving drinks and when all the customers are required by law to leave.

A tied house is owned by a brewery. A free house is owned by a private individual.

Tipsy is slightly drunk. Plastered is very, very drunk.

'The hard stuff' is Irish whiskey. 'A wee dram' is Scottish whisky.

Part three: Group work

**Unit 23
Leading the group**

1 Expressing opinions

Weak

► I would have thought . . .
► My impression is that . . .
► It seems to me that . . .

Strong

► I'm quite certain that . . .
► I don't doubt that . . .
► I feel sure that . . .

Asking for an opinion

► How does everyone feel about this?
► What's the general feeling about this?
► Any comments?
► Has anyone got any comments on that?
► Does anybody have any strong feelings on this?
► What does everyone think about this?
► What are everybody's views on that?
► Does anyone have any ideas on this?
► Well?

Medium

► I think . . .
► I don't think . . .
► I believe . . .
► As I see it . . . .
► It strikes me that . . .

Unit 24
Achieving
consensus

1 Government priorities — agreeing and disagreeing

Agreeing

- ► I agree completely.
- ► I couldn't agree more.
- ► Absolutely.
- ►*You're dead right there.

Expressing reservations

- ► Yes, but . . .
- ► Up to a point, but . . .
- ► Exactly, but don't you think that . . . ?
- ► You have a point there, but . . .

Agreeing tentatively

- ► I'm inclined to agree with you on that.
- ► I think I agree.
- ► I suppose that's true.

Being non-committal

- ► I wouldn't like to say.
- ► I can't say.

Disagreeing

- ►*Come off it.
- ► I'm sorry, but I really can't agree.
- ► I'm afraid I can't go along with you on that.
- ►*You must be joking.

* These colloquial expressions are used in informal situations amongst close friends.

'Perhaps' and 'You could be right' can be non-committal or show tentative agreement, depending on intonation.

Unit 25
Teamwork

2 Advice

'Your best bet is to . . . ' is colloquial.
'You should . . . ' and 'You'd better . . . ' are stronger and more forceful.
'Have you ever thought of . . . ?', 'Why don't you . . . ?' and 'You could always . . . ' are weaker.
Stronger forms are used for more serious problems.
'If I were you I **would** . . . '
'You **had** better . . . '

Unit 26
Decision-making

1 The board meeting

The phrases are similar because they are all used to advocate a plan of action, but the phrases for putting forward proposals are less common. Their use is limited to formal debates and meetings.

Accepting

- ► Yes, I'm in favour of that.
- ► That's got to be the best option/ solution.
- ► That's a very good idea.

Accepting reluctantly

- ► There doesn't seem to be much choice.
- ► We have no alternative.
- ► I suppose that's our only option.